Helping Your Child
Through Your Divorce

"A masterpiece in the critical area of divorce and custody."
— Frank S. Williams, M.D.
Director of Family and Child Psychiatry
at Cedars-Sinai Medical Center

"Illuminating case studies, sample agreements, charts, and clear, practical guidelines instruct and reassure . . . "
— *Library Journal*

". . . with this resource book, parents may find the help they need to navigate through the shoals of divorce to the post-divorce shared-parenting relationship that truly is in the best interests of the child."
— *Stepfamily Bulletin*

"This is a much-needed guidebook for concerned, loving parents who want to help their children before, during, and after a divorce. It is the ultimate expression of love for a parent to seek the education this book provides, then to follow its advice to the letter. Florence Bienenfeld has gathered, in one book, all the wisdom any parent needs to know during and after a divorce. As a therapist who has researched and worked with divorcing parents, I would heartily recommend this book to any parent in the midst of a divorce. *Helping Your Child Through Your Divorce* should be required reading for any divorced or divorcing parent."
— Doreen Virtue, Ph.D., Psychotherapist
Author, *My Kids Don't Live with Me Anymore: Coping with the Custody Crisis*

"In a 1987 mediation in Los Angeles, I requested Dr. Bienenfeld to co-mediate a seemingly irreconcilable custody issue. Both parents were entrenched in their positions and court proceedings seemed inevitable. Using her mediation skills, background and training in child development, and sensitive explanation of the children's pictures such as those in this book, Dr. Bienenfeld literally transformed the parents into collaborative, caring problem-solvers who negotiated a workable compromise that put the children's needs first and even improved their parental communication. As a professional colleague, Dr. Bienenfeld has earned my respect and admiration for her skills as a mediator and significant contributor to our professional literature."

— Forest F. Mosten, Family Law Attorney
and Mediator, Los Angeles, CA

"Getting a divorce when you have young children feels like being thrown into the sea. Your first thought is survival and it's hard to think about what is best for anyone else. Looking back now, I thank God for Florence's presence during the mediation session. She was like a life raft. She helped us both get out of our feelings about each other and concentrate on what we could do for our kids."

— A. M., Los Angeles, CA

"Within the last ten years, our family has experienced both mediation and the adversarial approach. Clearly, mediation is the alternative preferred by the children. As our family has certainly suffered from the adversarial situation, I wholeheartedly recommend the constructive interaction advocated by Dr. Bienenfeld, guiding all of us into a more loving relationship with our children."

— Dr. Arlene K. Magnus, Management Consultant,
Los Angeles, CA

Helping Your *Child*

Through Your *Divorce*

———

Florence Bienenfeld, Ph.D.

Foreword by Frank S. Williams, M.D.

Grateful acknowledgment is given for permission to reprint copyrighted material from: *My Mom and Dad are Getting a Divorce*
© 1980 EMC Corporation

Library of Congress Cataloging-in-Publication Data

Bienenfeld, Florence.
Helping your child through your divorce / Florence Bienenfeld.
p. cm.
Rev. ed. of: Helping your child succeed after divorce.
Includes bibliographical references and index.
ISBN 0-89793-174-2 (hard) : $21.95 — ISBN 0-89793-168-8 (pbk.) : $11.95
1. Children of divorced parents—United States. 2. Parent and child—United States. 3. Divorce—United States. I. Helping your child succeed after divorce.
II. Title.
HQ777.5.B54   1994
306.89—dc20   94-29255

Project editor: Lisa Lee   Production manager: Paul J. Frindt
Cover design: Madeleine Budnick Design   Cover photograph: Julian Okwu
Book design: Qalagraphia   Proofreader: Janet Eisen
Copy editors: Mali Apple, Elizabeth Bartelme
Sales & marketing: Corrine M. Sahli   Publicity & promotion: Darcy Cohan
Customer support: Sharon R. A. Olson, Sam Brewer
Order fulfillment: A & A Quality Shipping Services
Administration: María Jesús Aguiló
Publisher: Kiran S. Rana
Typeset in New Baskerville by 847 Communications, Alameda CA

9 8 7 6 5 4   Second revised edition

Ordering Information

Trade bookstores and wholesalers in the U.S. and Canada, please contact

Publishers Group West
1700 Fourth Street, Berkeley, CA 94710
telephone 800-788-3123 or 510-528-1444
fax 510-528-3444

Special sales

Hunter House books are available at special discounts when purchased
in bulk for sales promotions, premiums, or fundraising. For details,
please contact
Special Sales Department
Hunter House Inc.
P.O. Box 2914
Alameda CA 94501–0914
Telephone (510) 865-5282
Fax (510) 865-4295

College textbooks/course adoption orders

Please contact Hunter House at the address and phone
number above.

Orders by individuals or organizations

Hunter House books are available through most bookstores or can be
ordered directly from the publisher by calling toll-free

1-800-266-5592

Other Books by Florence Bienenfeld

Child Custody Mediation: Techniques for Counselors,
Attorneys, and Parents (1983)

My Mom and Dad Are Getting a Divorce (1980)

The Vegetarian Gourmet (1987)
(with Mickey Bienenfeld)

Healthy Baking (1992)
(with Mickey Bienenfeld)

Mother Nature's Garden (1994)
(with Mickey Bienenfeld)

Contents

To the many millions of children of divorce who look to their parents for care, guidance, reassurance, comfort, and love;

and

To their parents, who in spite of their own anger, anguish, and pain must nurture, protect, and help their children through their divorce.

Foreword

Dr. Florence Bienenfeld's book, written for parents of divorce, is a remarkable, well-coordinated contribution to the field of postdivorce counseling, mediation, and therapy. Dr. Bienenfeld's years of experience are reflected in her poignant and sensitive understanding and portrayal of the pain and anguish experienced by children, and their parents, going through divorce and postdivorce critical transitions.

This book should have a major impact on mental-health professionals, attorneys, mediators, and judges. I hope that it reaches a large number of these professionals, who come face to face with the war-torn child and adult victims of poorly handled separations and divorces.

The clinical examples given by Dr. Bienenfeld are precise and very much alive. They are appropriately shocking when they point to some very destructive attitudes that parents communicate to children as a result of their own pain and suffering. At other times, they display the chaotic world of children of divorce who are caught up in custody wars. Throughout, Dr. Bienenfeld maintains a down-to-earth, direct, and honest approach, which puts the examples in perspective. The children's drawings she has included, along with relevant familial data, bring to life the inner turmoil and suffering of children more effectively than anything I have seen before in print.

Dr. Bienenfeld's book points out the critical value of early intervention in helping parents achieve some measure of cooperation immediately after separation. She stresses the need for the parents to get off to a "good start" in an effort to avoid "the battles that may never end."

Dr. Bienenfeld addresses the most frequent battle issues in custody wars, incorporating examples and insights drawn from her own work with distraught parents. She covers many of the dilemmas and pitfalls in child-custody arrangements, with practical approaches and advice for situations ranging from what to say and how to handle feared sexual abuse, conflicts with grandparents, holiday schedules, great geographical distance between parents, a parent being gay, and anxieties over a stepparent or other significant person in the other parent's life. Her insightful responses to some of these universal and ofttimes delicate perplexities in divorced families center on bringing significant structure and order into the shattered world of children of divorce. Her advice aims at developing a sense of security and an organized life pattern for the children. She points out how structure, security, and ongoing meaningful contact with both parents can replace fear, turmoil, and depression.

Dr. Bienenfeld's book includes an excellent description of how mediation can and does work. Her vivid descriptions of actual mediation cases again underline how she keeps the process focused on the needs of the children, and demonstrates how she includes children in the mediation process.

Congratulations to Dr. Bienenfeld for what I consider to be a masterpiece in the critical area of divorce and custody. Dr. Bienenfeld's book should establish once and for all that children of divorce need frequent and ongoing contact with both parents. And while reinforcing her emphasis, I would like to add that parents as well as professionals in our field need frequent and ongoing contact with Dr. Florence Bienenfeld's very fine book.

Frank S. Williams, M.D.

Frank S. Williams, M.D., is the Director of Family and Child Psychiatry at Cedars-Sinai Medical Center in Los Angeles, and is a member of the California State Bar Association Standing Committee on Child Custody and Visitation. Dr. Williams and the mental-health staff he trains and supervises are considered leading experts in custody evaluations, and regularly consult to the Los Angeles County Family Law Conciliation Court. They carry out a large number of the court- and attorney-referred custody evaluations for Los Angeles County Superior Court and Orange County Superior Court.

Preface

If I were to ask your child what he or she wants to see happen after divorce, most likely your child would answer, "I want my mom and dad to get back together again, but if they can't, at least I wish they could be friends." In sharp contrast, if I were to ask divorcing parents the same question, most would answer that they want to have nothing at all to do with the other parent.

How children do in life after a divorce depends to a large degree on how their parents behave and on their parents' attitudes toward each other.

Although each divorce and custody situation is unique, there are common problems and concerns that may face many of you and your children. The family situations I describe here are real ones. I have changed names and other identifying material to preserve confidentiality.

The purpose of my book is to help you, the divorcing parent, create a safe and nurturing environment for your children after divorce. Only then can your children recover and heal, then blossom and succeed. The practical information, concepts, insights, examples, and suggestions in the book can serve as a guide to raising successful and happy children after divorce. This result is within your reach.

You have my empathy, warmest regards, and best wishes. This is a very difficult period for you personally, and it will take you time to recover and heal yourself. But remember, what you do to help your children today will create a brighter tomorrow for them—and for you.

Florence Bienenfeld
California, 1994

Acknowledgments

I wish to express my appreciation to Frank S. Williams, M.D., for reviewing my book and for his thoughtful foreword.

I would also like to express my gratitude to the late Meyer Elkin, former Director of Conciliation Court of Los Angeles County; Hugh McIsaac, former Director of Conciliation Court of Los Angeles County and present Director, Family Court Services, Multnomah County, Oregon; and E. Ronald Hulbert, Ph.D., psychologist, former Supervisor of Training, Research and Staff Development, Conciliation Court of Los Angeles County, and present Division Chief Child Custody Evaluations, Administratively Unified Court of Los Angeles County, for reviewing and endorsing this book.

A special thanks to Carl Whitaker, M.D., Professor of Psychiatry, Center for Health Sciences, University of Wisconsin Madison, for endorsing and writing the foreword for my book, *Child Custody Mediation* (1983), now out of print. Some of the valuable materials on mediation contained in that book have been incorporated into the revised text of this one.

I wish to thank Kiran Rana, Lisa Lee, and all the fine staff at Hunter House for their expertise and support.

A special acknowledgment is due Isolina Ricci, Ph.D., statewide Coordinator of Family Court Services for Judicial Council of California. Her pioneering work since the early 1970s, and her book *Mom's House, Dad's House*, have greatly influenced the thinking, attitudes, and even the language of parenting after divorce.

A very special word of appreciation is offered to the thousands of parents and children I have counseled, along with my best wishes to them all.

Last but not least, I wish to acknowledge and thank my loving and caring husband, Mickey; our three wonderful children and their spouses; and our growing number of adorable grandchildren, all of whom bring me such warmth and joy.

1

Making Wise Decisions

When a boat is sinking, all the passengers are given life preservers. When a marriage comes to an end, a similar state of emergency exists, but no one hands you a life preserver. You, your children, and the other parent are on your own, thrashing about, trying hard to survive. Many parents in this situation feel like helpless, frightened children themselves, wishing someone or something would save them.

Imagine, then, how devastated and powerless children feel. A separation and divorce is a shocking experience for them, for their very existence depends on their parents. They sustain tremendous losses and experience great pain before, during, and after divorce. The crisis and tragedy of divorce is that this time, when parents are usually least able to help or even think about helping, is when children need their help most of all. In fact, if your child is to succeed after divorce, he or she will need your *utmost* help.

Helping Children Succeed

What I mean by the term "to succeed" is to turn out well, prosper, accomplish, thrive, and flourish. A child needs to make a good recovery from the trauma of divorce to do well in school; to be happy, relaxed, and satisfied; and to have a strong sense of self as well as a good self-image. Most important, a child needs to be able to love, to have good relationships, and eventually to be able to sustain positive intimate relationships in adulthood.

To help children achieve this success, divorcing parents must make wise decisions *jointly* at a time when it is extremely difficult for them to even communicate or cooperate. Many parents are so upset and in so much pain that they are unwilling or unable to focus on what their children need. Without realizing it, they may hurt their own children unmercifully.

The purpose of my book is to help parents create a nurturing environment for their children in spite of their own pain, so that their children will recover from the divorce, heal, and feel good about themselves and their lives. To accomplish this I offer encouragement, information, knowledge, and practical ideas that can help parents minimize the stress, pain, and loss for their children. Specific examples will help divorcing parents develop a suitable parenting plan, avoid hassles and arguments, and settle disagreements. I have also provided guidelines for handling many common situations, such as dealing with emergencies, deciding when your child needs outside help, and finding ways to settle disputes when parenting practices differ.

If parents are in too much pain to work out such issues on their own, mediation can and should be used to help resolve conflicts. Resources for finding help of various kinds are included in Chapter 10, *Where to Find Help*, and in the suggested reading list of books written for divorcing parents and their children.

Over a ten-year period as Senior Family Mediator/Counselor for the Conciliation Court of Los Angeles County, and for an additional ten years as a marriage, family, and child counselor in private practice, I have counseled thousands of divorcing parents and their children. Mothers and fathers have tearfully told me about their pain and problems; their anguish, concerns, frustrations, anger, bitterness, disappointment, and mistrust; and their fears. They have discussed their thoughts, beliefs, and attitudes, as well as their desires and dreams for their children.

Most parents mean well, but some feel too threatened and too blinded by their own pain to think clearly and to make wise decisions regarding their children. Many are themselves struggling to work through their painful childhood experiences and do not see how they are sentencing their children to repeat the same behaviors. Children learn about life from their experiences with their parents and from the way their parents behave and get along with one another. They tend to repeat patterns they are familiar with, even when those patterns are destructive, and in this way behaviors are passed from one generation to another.

At a time like this, you and your children need all the help and support possible. No matter how difficult, strained, or miserable your relationship with the other parent has been in the past, it is not too late to begin working together to help your children. Their emotional and physical health lie in your hands. If children are unhappy as children, it is unlikely they will be happy as adults. It is up to you as parents to protect them from unnecessary pain and to create a secure and nurturing environment. Children need parental cooperation and all the love they can get from both of their parents, and from their grandparents, stepparents, relatives, and friends.

The three most important steps you can take to help your child succeed are to develop a closer relationship with your child; to relate more positively to the other parent; and to share parenting after the divorce. If you free your child from parental conflict and allow him or her to enjoy a close and loving relationship with both parents, you will be giving your child a greater possibility of happiness—by far the best gift you can give, and by far the best way you can show your love.

The Pain of Divorce

Difficult as a divorce is for parents, it is truly devastating for children, since they are completely dependent on their parents. Often, they do not know what is happening, and the guessing and uncertainty create traumas that may surface and demand attention much later in life. Many children never get to voice their pain, anger, and frustration in the way their parents do. As a result, they tend to feel extremely helpless, isolated, and confused. Still, children are remarkably resilient. Although they experience great pain and feelings of loss, most children can and will recover if their parents allow them to heal.

For many children, the greater pain comes *after* the divorce. Approximately one-third of the children of divorce lose contact with one of their parents, and untold numbers of children are tormented as parents continue to do battle long after the divorce is final. Frequently children become the focal point for the arguments and bitterness. Parental hostility often escalates through the years, causing needless pain and suffering all around.

What this does to children psychologically is not hard to imagine. The longer the parental conflict continues and the greater the tension, the greater the likelihood that serious psychological damage will result. Some children protect themselves by turning off their feelings: they no longer feel pain, but neither do they feel other emotions, not even pleasant ones. In short, they become emotional zombies.

If they are continually exposed to intense pain and loss, children tend to experience negative feelings about themselves, about others, and about life in general. They become reluctant to risk loving other people for fear of being hurt again, and these negative attitudes work against happy and satisfying lives.

According to Drs. Judith Wallerstein and Joan B. Kelly, who conducted a ten-year study of children of divorce, if children are deprived of one of their parents, or if their parents quarrel and compete, children tend to have lower self-esteem. Psychological damage often occurs, and children may develop such serious symptoms as anxiety, depression, regression, sleep disturbances including nightmares and sleepwalking, asthma, allergies, bedwetting, tantrums, and tics. They may grind their teeth, vomit, become clinging or overaggressive, begin daydreaming, or withdraw from relationships. Overeating or loss of appetite, poor school performance, delinquent behavior, self-destructive behavior, alcohol or drug abuse, frequent crying or absence of emotion, and difficulty in communicating feelings are other symptoms. Professional counseling should be sought if any of these symptoms persist.

It is not uncommon for parents to get off to a bad start at the separation and get locked into a negative way of regarding each other. They may try to get even with and punish each other for their pain. They may feel hurt and wounded, refusing to work together to help their children. When one parent tries to punish the other, it is the children who are punished and hurt most of all.

Hundreds of thousands of children in the United States are involved in custody battles each year. They often become victims of a legal system that promotes competition rather than cooperation between parents. Warring parents go into court trying to "win" their children, and during the battle children are often pressured to take sides or asked to choose where they want to live—putting them in a no-win situation.

Battles over child custody tend to increase hostility between parents, thus lessening the possibility of later cooperation. Some battles continue for years, and children suffer tremendously. One sixteen-year-old boy, whose parents had been in court every year since he was six, told me, "I'm so disgusted that I have lost all my feeling for my parents." A twenty-one-year-old woman, whose parents divorced when she was twelve, said, "I remember freaking out in the judge's chambers when he asked me who I wanted to live with. I told him I wanted to live with my dad because my mother was moving away and I didn't want to leave my friends. It made me feel terrible to have to choose, but everything is fine now, except that I have a terrible attitude about marriage. I don't think that will ever change."

Even when parents are upset and in pain themselves, it is essential that they consider their children. Children should not be kept waiting until parents finally get their lives together. They need at least a tolerable situation in which they can recover from the divorce.

Child-Custody Mediation

Mediation is a way of avoiding much of the pain of divorce. This powerful process can help parents resolve their problems out of court; moreover, it gives parents the power to make their own decisions, instead of having a judge make them. Child-custody mediation offers parents the opportunity to meet with a trained, neutral, third-party, who helps them discuss their issues, concerns, and differences in a nonadversarial setting. They are helped to focus on their children's needs and on the present instead of the past, and they explore various alternatives for resolving their differences. When they are able to reach an agreement, the mediator assists them in writing it up so that it can later be made into a legal and binding court order.

Mediation attempts to reduce the hostility between parents and to effect a more positive outcome for the children. I believe very strongly in the mediation process, and I will give here a brief description of how I use it. (See Chapter 8, *Child-Custody Mediation* for more detailed information.)

I see both parents together. After I explain the purpose of mediation, I structure the interview so that each parent has a chance to tell me how he or she sees the situation and what he or she wants to see happen. I encourage parents to talk about their concerns, feelings, and needs. Then I spend a few moments putting what they have said into perspective, and educating them about the needs of children in general and the developmental needs of their children in particular. I try to make communication between parents easier, and I assist them in discussing issues, focusing on their children's needs and looking at a range of alternatives. When parents are willing, I help them draft a parenting agreement that can meet their children's needs and the family's needs as a whole. If attorneys have accompanied the parents, they are included at the beginning and at the end of the session.

During the mediation process, much of my time is spent interviewing children and counseling entire families. My experience has been that children benefit tremendously from being included in the mediation process; the difference in their faces, attitudes, voices, and body language from the time they first walk into my office to the time they leave is observable and dramatic.

Some parents and professionals believe it is best not to include children in the mediation process because they might become upset, but these children are usually upset already. They often have no neutral person to talk to about their feelings, and many children carry feelings of loss, sadness, and frustration over into adulthood.

Including children in the mediation process gives them an opportunity to speak, to be heard, and to gain perspective about the difficult situation in which they find themselves. Most children leave the mediation session *less* burdened and better fortified for whatever may happen to them. It also gives parents an opportunity to hear and see how much anguish their competition causes children. Some parents can then focus more on their children's needs and less on their own positions, and are more apt to cooperate with one another in negotiating a suitable parenting agreement.

Even when children are not included in the mediation process directly, they benefit tremendously from the help and education their parents receive. The intervention often comes at a time when adults are too upset to deal clearly with all the different demands of the situation.

One key to helping parents settle their differences is having sufficient time to work with them. It is essential that both parents have the chance to be heard, and that sufficient time be allowed to discuss the situation fully and to explore all feasible alternatives. Occasionally, follow-up phone calls or seeing each parent alone can have positive results. When there is a stalemate, I often find that including the children and providing feedback to the parents helps them to recognize their children's needs and thus reach an agreement.

To make a child-custody agreement an enforceable and binding legal document, it must be written up, signed by both parents and by a family law judge or commissioner, and filed with the court. It is then a court order, and should a parent refuse to comply with it, the other parent has legal recourse and may file contempt charges.

Before matters escalate to this point, parents have the opportunity of airing their grievances to a court mediator or private mediator. At that time parents can talk to each other about their difficulties and can modify their agreement, if they are able to agree on the changes. Considering the difficulty of the divorce mediation cases I see, it is amazing that an agreement rate of more than 70 percent has been possible. These agreements tend to hold over time, and most of these parents do not return to court unless new problems arise.

The best possible result from mediation is that parents reach a suitable agreement regarding how they will parent their children after divorce. Ideally, their plan meets their children's specific needs and makes sense for all concerned. However, even when parents do not reach an agreement, the mediation process has usually encouraged them to focus on their children's needs and has exposed them to insights and alternatives they may consider in the future. Creating a better outcome for the children *is* the purpose of mediation.

Parenting After Divorce

Much of the anger and futility experienced by adults after a divorce stems from what happened during the marriage or events that took place at the time of separation. For many individuals, the months just prior to and after separation are an extremely difficult time. Emotions are raw, and parents tend to blame each other for the breakup. During these stormy periods, parents sometimes do and say terrible things to each other, often quite oblivious to the pain their behavior is causing their children. It is difficult for many men and women to separate "husband-wife" issues from "mother-father" issues. They do not realize that although divorce ends their marriage, it does not end their parental relationship.

Young children do not understand adult problems. They do not know what happened or why one parent has left. They are confused and bewildered, and sometimes they believe that the parent who stays loves them more than the one who has gone. In reality, the one who leaves may have been ordered to go and be truly miserable about being away from them.

Children take divorce hard, for they are extremely attached to both parents. Most children want their parents to stay together; when their parents separate, it knocks the props right out from under them. Children, as well as adults, go through a classical mourning process after divorce, much as if someone close to them has died. First they experience disbelief; then anxiety, anger, sadness, and depression; and eventually, if given reassurance, acceptance of the divorce and healing. This process can take a year or longer. If they are ever to recover, to feel secure, and to succeed, they need to be told, to believe, and to feel that their mother and father both love them and have every intention of continuing to take care of them, even though they now live apart.

No matter what has gone on between the parents, children have a strong need to look up to and to maintain a good relationship with each of them. They need frequent and ongoing contact with both parents, who must be willing to put aside their own hurt and anger and cooperate in setting up a workable parenting schedule. Frequent and regular contact with both parents can make children feel secure and prevent them from thinking they have been rejected and abandoned.

Most of all, children desperately need parental cooperation after divorce. They need two parents who are willing to work together as partners, even if they do not like each other or are not friends. Parents should take to heart and follow these six principles:

1. Stop blaming the other parent or yourself for what happened in the past. Realize that the past is behind you and cannot be relived.

2. Realize that your child needs *two* parents. Be willing to share your child with the other parent.

3. In your discussions with the other parent, stick to issues pertaining to your child.

4. Stay focused on your child's needs today and from now on.

5. Work together with the other parent to provide your child with as safe and as conflict-free an environment as possible.

6. Make every effort to be civil to your former spouse, and defuse tension and animosity so that your child can have a peaceful and satisfying life.

If you feel you need help, it is an act of love and caring and a sign of strength to seek appropriate assistance for yourself and your children. The children's drawings in Chapter 2, *How Children See Divorce,* poignantly reveal how deeply some of them experience parental conflict and how much they need to be helped. When you ask for and receive help, you may rediscover the world through the eyes of a child, and you will likely be touched inside.

You now have it in your power to correct what was wrong in the past and to build a good life for yourself and for your children. As you watch your children blossom, you will know it was well worth it. Think about how good you will feel if your child is able to look back some day and say, "I had a good childhood. My parents both loved me very much." It is the best launching pad you can give your children for their flight through life. The chain of unhappiness will be broken, and your life will be happier, too. So be strong, and be of good courage: your children are counting on you.

2

How Children See Divorce

The drawings in this chapter dramatically illustrate how children experience divorce. In them you will see pain and conflict, as well as disbelief, confusion, anxiety, anger, frustration, guilt, sadness, hopelessness, powerlessness, despair, and love. Some children express wishes and fantasies, usually the wish that their family will be reunited, that peace and harmony will be restored, or that there might be an end to the fighting. These poignant drawings reveal the depth of these children's feelings, and illustrate how much children are in touch with the main issues and how they try to handle and integrate their experiences.

These drawings were made in the waiting room outside my office by children involved in custody or visitation disputes. No suggestion whatsoever was given by me to the children as to what to draw. I merely asked each of them if they wanted to draw a picture while they were waiting. If they showed an interest, I gave them crayons and a few sheets of plain paper. I did not question them about their drawings afterward, though some children volunteered comments about what they were portraying. From hundreds of pictures, I have selected these as examples of the responses children have to the stress of divorce and parental conflict.

Each drawing is accompanied by some factual and anecdotal information, which has been disguised to maintain confidentiality. The children's names are also fictitious.

Children's art, as well as their stories, fantasies, dreams, and play, can be therapeutic tools and excellent for discovering children's inner worlds. I have purposely done little psychological interpretation of these drawings, as each is self-explanatory, telling its own story.

These children, and untold numbers like them, are involved in intolerable situations that can only lead to frustration and unhappiness. Many are in no-win situations that keep them in a state of torment throughout their childhood. To make matters worse, the quality of their lives does not improve in adulthood because of the unhappy memories and experiences they carry with them.

The positive side to all of this is that parents can learn to get along after divorce and that children are resilient and can heal rather quickly if given a chance. I hope these drawings will inspire parents to work together cooperatively so their children can feel good about their lives and the chain of unhappiness can be broken forever.

The drawings on the first few pages illustrate how some children experience a divorce and subsequent custody dispute as a disaster.

Two Houses Under the Ocean

Bruce drew two houses at the bottom of the ocean. Overhead, a submarine is dropping torpedoes on the houses. He wrote the word *divorce* in jagged letters across the top.

Bruce's parents had recently separated and were constantly arguing in front of Bruce and his sister. Each parent felt threatened that he or she could lose everything, including the children. They were both extremely upset and seemed oblivious to the pain they were causing Bruce and his sister.

It is easy for divorcing parents to lose sight of their children's feelings and needs when they are devastated and overwhelmed themselves. But, especially at this time, children experience parental arguments and conflicts as very frightening and confusing. This, coupled with a divorce, can be devastating. It shakes their inner security system to the core, leaving them weaker and less likely to succeed in whatever they undertake in life.

Drawing by Bruce, age 9

Divorce Is What Makes the World Fall Apart

Bruce's sister Eileen literally drew a world cut in two. Eileen expressed her belief that divorce is what makes the world fall apart, and she views the bad part as much bigger than the good part. Her parent's arguments undoubtedly contributed heavily to making her world seem that way.

During a divorce, it is not unusual for parents also to feel as if their world is falling apart. It usually does collapse on many levels: financial, emotional, social. And in the middle of everything there are the children to raise.

Children are obliged to live in the kind of world their parents create for them. Cooperation and effective communication between parents are needed to help children experience their world as a *good* and *safe* place to live.

Drawing by Eileen, age 10

A FAMILY STRUCK BY LIGHTNING

Jill drew bolts of lightning striking her family.

Jill had been away at summer camp when her parents separated. Coming home, she was suddenly faced with not only a divorce but also a custody battle. To her this was as shocking as lightning striking her family.

Children should be prepared in advance for a separation or divorce whenever possible, and arrangements should be made for frequent contact with both parents. The children should be assured that they will be well taken care of and loved by both parents even after the separation, and that the divorce will not mean disaster for them.

Drawing by Jill, age 11

Doomsday

Dana drew what appeared to be a nuclear holocaust, with ghosts lurking everywhere. Her drawing has an eerie, dismal quality. Dana's parents had divorced many years earlier, but their bitterness remained. As a result of this bitterness, Dana had not seen her father for many years. By the time he took her mother to court for visiting rights, Dana refused to see him.

Some parents nurse resentments and bitterness from their marriage for many years after a divorce, allowing it to erode the quality of their children's and their own lives. Harboring resentments and grudges wastes an individual's energy and vitality. Counseling and therapy can help people free themselves from past pain.

Children who lose contact or become estranged from one of their parents suffer deep feelings of abandonment, depression, despair, and low self-esteem.

Drawing by Dana, age 11

The next two drawings express the confusion and disorientation many children feel.

THE WHIRLWIND

The whirlwind of confusion depicted in this drawing parallels the current life of Ryan, who is involved in a whirlwind-like custody battle. Ryan told me that he felt caught in the middle and "that doesn't feel good."

Divorcing parents often compete and fight over their children because they feel insecure themselves. They insist on having their children to themselves instead of sharing them. They do not realize that neither parent owns the children, and that parents are merely given the privilege and opportunity of raising them.

Children like Ryan become anxious, insecure, and confused when their parents fight over them.

Drawing by Ryan, age 8

Floating in Space

Tallia expresses great insecurity in this drawing. Instead of being grounded, she draws herself as a large, bodiless head with tiny legs floating in space in the upper-left corner of her drawing.

Tallia's mother was extremely upset after the separation and made it difficult for their father to see the children. He became frustrated and angry, threatening to take the children from her. Tallia's mother panicked and kept the children from seeing their father; he responded by snatching them from her. During and after the divorce, Tallia and her younger brother were snatched back and forth several times. This is one of the most frightening and damaging experiences for a child. Tallia's disorientation and insecurity are apparent in her drawing.

Child-snatching is a felony under federal law. A parent who has difficulty seeing a child may feel justified in taking that child away, but should resist the temptation for the child's sake and to avoid even more serious problems in the future. It is far better for such parents to settle their problems by legal means or by mediation. For how to find child-custody mediation services, see Chapter 10, *Where to Find Help*.

No matter how upset parents are, they must avoid causing their children the kind of pain evident in this drawing.

Drawing by Tallia, age 6

Some children express how torn they feel and the extreme pressure they are under during a custody dispute.

WHICH WAY SHALL I GO?

In this drawing, Mark depicts himself standing on top of a rainbow arched over two houses. Mark explained, "My parents are sliding down the rainbow into separate houses. I don't know which way to go. My legs are sticking out in both directions because I don't know which way to go."

At the time Mark made this drawing, he and his parents were still living in the family home. His drawing shows concern about having to choose between his parents once they separate. Mark's father was taking the divorce very hard; he was worried that he would lose his son the way he had lost his own father when he was five. Both parents were asking Mark to live with them.

In mediation, Mark's parents were able to agree on a shared-parenting plan in which Mark would spend more or less equal amounts of time with each of them. Mark's parents had addressed Mark's needs by being willing to share him rather than continuing to compete for him.

Drawing by Mark, age 9

THEY'RE BOTH COMING TO HUG ME

This drawing was also made by Mark. He explained its meaning to me by saying, "My mom and dad are both coming to hug me. I don't know which one to hug first."

Mark tries hard to please both his parents. I gave him some simple advice: "Don't worry about which one to hug first. Just hug one and then hug the other."

Drawing by Mark, age 9

THE PITS

In this drawing, Joseph, a gifted child, depicts himself as a stick figure hanging from a ladder suspended between two hills. He labeled the void below him "The Pits." On one hill he wrote to his dad, "I love you!" His father is telling him, "I'll give you a motorcycle." On the other hill he wrote to his mother, "I love you, too!" His mother is telling him: "Come with me, we'll have a lot of fun."

When I spoke with him, Joseph said, "My dad says my mom's not being a good mom and he wants me to come and live with him. My mom says she is a good mom, so they're going to court. I feel bad. It puts me and my sister in the middle."

Divorce tug-of-wars are extremely painful for children. Joseph's father had not been very involved in Joseph's life for many years following the divorce. After he remarried and was expecting another child, he wanted custody of Joseph and his sister, he said, to make up for all the time he had lost. Joseph's mother was against this: "I had to raise them alone, now he wants them." She wanted to punish him for his neglect. I encouraged her to let the father be more involved, even if he had not been in the past. That was what her children needed now.

In mediation, Joseph and his sister expressed their deep desire to spend more time with their father. Their parents settled on a shared-parenting plan that allowed the children equal time with both parents. Joseph and his sister were very pleased. They got their wish, and the pressure was off at last.

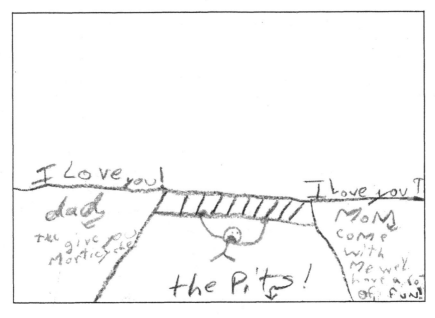

Drawing by Joseph, age 11

FIVE DAISIES STANDING IN A ROW

Christina, Joseph's sister and also a gifted child, depicts her family as five daisies standing in a row. She colored her mother's and stepfather's petals orange, her father's and stepmother's petals purple, and her own petals half orange and half purple. She fashioned the green leaves as hearts.

She told me, "The reason my father wants me to come and live with him is because my stepmother is expecting a baby, and so he wouldn't have to pay child support if I went to live with him." She had heard her mother talking about it. "We couldn't go to my dad's house because he didn't pay child support."

She said she worries, "because if I go with my mother, my dad will be sad. If I go with my dad, my mother will be sad and this problem makes me feel sad."

Included as part of the agreement reached by the parents in mediation was a statement restraining them from making any derogatory remarks about each other in the presence of their children. I received feedback more than a year later that they were keeping to their agreements—a loving gift indeed for their children.

Drawing by Christina, age 9

Some children express strong anger, frustration, and guilt in their drawings. Frequently, the anger they portray is from one parent or both.

THE PRISONER

Joey drew himself as a prisoner with a ball and chain. He was involved in an exceptionally guilt-producing custody dispute. Since his parents' separation and divorce, he had been living with an invalid mother who relied on Joey more and more for help and care. Joey begged his mother to let him live with his father so he could be free to pursue sports and other activities, but Joey's mother would not give him permission to leave.

Joey's mother needed someone to care for her, but if Joey continued to be burdened with her care, he would be deprived of what he needed as a developing boy.

Family counseling can help in complex situations. In this family, one of the goals would be to help Joey and his parents deal with Joey's anger and guilt; another would be to help Joey's mother find suitable help and care.

Drawing by Joey, age 11

THE BIRD

During a family counseling session, Scott's mother was openly hostile toward his father in Scott's presence. I noticed a striking resemblance between the bird Scott had drawn and his mother. The resemblance had to do with her facial expression and the way she opened her mouth when she spoke angrily against his father. Scott's mother refused to restrain her anger at his father in front of Scott even when I asked her to.

Some parents are so angry with the other parent that they lash out with bitter words. Parents need to get their anger out, but in appropriate ways, and *not* in front of their children.

Counseling and therapy can help parents release hostility and regain control. Otherwise, the children get caught in the middle of the conflict and become helpless and angry themselves. Some children resent a parent who makes angry remarks and find it increasingly difficult to be with that parent. Other children come to believe what the hostile parent says and refuse to see the other parent. Some children become hostile toward both parents. No matter which way it goes, the children are the losers.

Drawing by Scott, age 12

Bloody Monster

Chris drew an angry monster and pointed out the dripping blood. His mother had run away with Chris when he was a year old and had gone into hiding. The child did not see his father and three sisters for ten years. When he was eleven, he found out how to get in touch with his father, and now he refuses to see his mother in spite of her remorse for the unfair thing she did to him.

Chris's mother had felt so trapped and unhappy in her marriage that when she had left, ten years before, all she could think of was getting out—not seeking help. She had no money and nowhere to go, so she left the three older children with their father, took the baby, and ran.

During an interview, Chris said sadly, "I hate life sometimes. I should have been able to see my sisters. I get real angry at my mom and dad. Sometimes I'm mad at the whole world."

Chris may eventually forgive his mother, or he may carry his unresolved anger into adulthood and allow it to severely hamper his adult relationships. His sisters will likely have immense feelings of abandonment to deal with.

I encouraged family counseling for the entire family, to help Chris and his sisters work through their pain and to help the parents resolve their differences.

Drawing by Chris, age 11

Some drawings show how hard some children try not to feel anything.

An Armored Armadillo

Bobby sat rigidly guarded during his individual interview. He expressed little emotion when he said he was used to his parents' arguing and that he didn't care what happened.

When pain becomes extreme and continues over a long period of time, some children protect themselves with a coat of armor much like that of the armadillo in Bobby's drawing. If the conflict continues without relief, these children may remain armored and unfeeling throughout their lives, experiencing neither pain nor pleasure nor love.

It is often difficult for divorcing parents to act civilly toward each other, but if they want their children to grow into loving, caring, feeling people, they *must* create a tolerable situation for them when they are young.

Drawing by Bobby, age 7

Some children take sides with one parent and express this polarization in their drawings.

THE FAMILY DIVIDED

Tami drew a picture of herself standing next to her mother. She explained that her drawing meant that her older sister wanted to live with their father, but that she and her younger sister wanted to live with their mother. Here is a family truly divided, with one child choosing to be separated from her sisters in order not to leave one of the divorcing parents.

Following separation and divorce, there is a real risk of children losing a close relationship with one of their parents. Parents can help prevent this by encouraging the children to spend time with the other parent. Children need to feel that they have a home with both parents.

Drawing by Tami, age 8

Some children express fear in their drawings.

GHOSTS

Erick drew a house surrounded by scary ghosts. During our interview, he told me how scared he had been when his mother's boyfriend had held him by his heels and stuck his head in the toilet
while his mother stood by and did nothing. "Because I wouldn't
flush it," he explained.

In this situation, Erick's mother may have been so frightened
and insecure herself, and so desperate for a relationship with her
boyfriend, that she allowed her son to be traumatized and abused
by him. She is not unique, for there are insecure parents who know
that their children are being sexually molested and do nothing to
stop it out of fear of losing a relationship with the molester. Other
parents abuse their own children, and they themselves may have
been abused as children.

*Children must be protected from being abused physically and emotion-
ally.* Harsh punishments and threats of punishment should be
avoided. Although these punishments might appear to bring about
better behavior, they can cause serious psychological harm. Parents
should look for other ways to discipline their children, and they
might find help in professional counseling, available in most communities through mental-health and family-service agencies.

If, for any reason, a parent cannot provide a safe environment
for his or her children, that parent should seek another living situation for them. He or she might encourage the child to live with the
other parent until the situation improves, or seek other emergency
help (see Chapter 10, *Where to Find Help*).

Drawing by Erick, age 6

Many children express a great sadness in their drawings.

A Sad Clown

Lori had not seen her father much since the separation. After her father married a woman with two children of her own, Lori felt very left out and alone. She longed to have her father to herself sometimes, but her stepmother wouldn't hear of it.

In her drawing, Lori's depiction of herself as a sad clown is a reflection of the sadness she was experiencing. Some children experience tremendous feelings of loss, sadness, depression, rejection, and abandonment when they get less special attention from a parent who has remarried.

At the same time, Lori's stepmother was also feeling insecure and left out on the weekends that Lori came to visit. She looked forward to spending time alone with her husband on weekends, since they both worked all week.

Two or three hours alone with a parent can often satisfy children, and it may not be necessary to exclude the stepparent for long periods. I often suggest a breakfast or early dinner in a restaurant for the mother or father and the child, or a picnic or walk or other activity during the week as an alternative to time alone on the weekend.

Drawing by Lori, age 11

The Good Times and the Bummers

Linda's parents had been separated several months. Both her younger sister and she said they did not want to live with either parent because of the terrible fights their parents were having over money. They asked to be able to live with a cousin for a while until their parents settled their financial squabbles. After Linda made this drawing, I asked whether her life was a good time or a bummer. She replied sadly, "Mostly bummers."

Many parents go through a very stormy period before and after separation, and during that period they find it difficult to control their behavior. The two faces Linda drew clearly indicate the emotional ups and downs she had been through. Her sadness and confusion may have been avoided if her parents had kept their quarrels private.

Drawing by Linda, age 12

Some children describe through their drawing what is happening in their lives and what they want to happen.

THIS IS HOW I FEEL AND THIS IS WHAT IS HAPPENING

Amy drew a picture of herself standing in a rainstorm with a big frown on her face. Her wish, she told me, was that her parents would stop fighting. When her mother and father reached an agreement, Amy was ecstatic. "I got my wish!" she said joyously.

Unfortunately, this was not the end of her parents' conflicts. Two years later Amy made a second drawing, which showed her parents arguing over Amy. Though it was done in cartoon fashion, it was not funny. Amy stated clearly that she did not want her parents to argue when her mother came to pick her up.

Parents who remain connected or bonded in a negative way after a divorce continue to go round and round, never ending their conflict or freeing themselves to live happily. When these battles continue year after year, a child can be tormented. Such parents owe it to themselves and to their children to seek individual help or postdivorce counseling (see Chapter 8, *Child-Custody Mediation*).

Drawings by Amy, age 8,
and Amy, age 10

Some children express their feelings of powerlessness through their artwork.

RULER OF THE MOUNTAIN

Ricky is another child who was snatched back and forth by his parents. First his mother took him, and he did not see his father for years; then his father snatched him, and his mother vanished from his life. Ricky was young and powerless.

In his drawing, Ricky reveals his deep wish to be *powerful*. He depicts himself as "ruler of the highest mountain," a powerful being indeed. Some children who feel powerless in their youth never shed their feeling of impotence as they grow into adulthood.

Violence between parents, threats of violence, and feelings of extreme insecurity can lead some parents to take off with the children. This leads to retaliation by the other parent, and the children are caught in the middle.

Only parents can give children the power of security they long for. Parents who are feeling threatened can find help without putting their children through the pain of life as fugitives.

Drawing by Ricky, age 12

Some drawings show a child's secret desire for contact with a parent.

DADDY, LOOK, A PUPPY

Tammy told me she did not want to see her father because he was not paying child support and had left her mother for another woman. Tammy's choice of words, her tone of voice, and her facial expressions mirrored her mother's. In spite of Tammy's angry words, in her drawing she depicted herself as having a friendly interaction with her father, telling him, "Daddy, look, a puppy." Her father's response is, "We'll name it Dusty."

Children like Tammy long for a close relationship with both parents but are forced to take sides with a hostile parent because they are afraid they will lose that parent's love.

Tammy's mother meant Tammy no harm. She felt so betrayed by and bitter toward Tammy's father that she thought only about how she could hurt him back. She was not thinking about Tammy's need to have a father.

I pointed out the harm she was causing Tammy and how her behavior could destroy Tammy's chances for a happy life. Fortunately, she understood. She agreed that Tammy could begin spending weekends with her father and that she would take Tammy to family counseling. Tammy looked amazed and relieved when she found out she could see her father on weekends. I give her mother a lot of credit for being willing to listen and to change her attitude and behavior.

Drawing by Tammy, age 8

Some children recall the past through their drawings.

WHEN MY DADDY WAS LIVING HERE

Sara remembers a time when her parents were living together. In her drawing, she tells the story of how her sister poured cereal all over the floor when her father was living with them.

Children tend to hold on to memories of how life was before the divorce. Since children do not understand adult problems, some blame themselves or their siblings for the breakup. *Children should be told that they did not cause the divorce.* They should be given a simple explanation for what happened—an explanation that blames neither parent.

It takes courage for parents to be honest and to acknowledge their own part in what has happened in their lives. It is often much easier to blame the other parent, even though that makes the divorce much harder on the children.

Drawing by Sara, age 10

Some children express fantasies in their drawings that deny the reality of the divorce.

FAMILY WITH BALLOONS

Ellie's parents had separated recently. They told me that Ellie had been very upset by the separation. In her drawing, Ellie depicted her family standing in a row, with her mother next to her father, and her brother and herself holding balloons, as if her family were on a joyous outing and the separation had never happened.

Disbelief or denial is the first stage in the long grieving process. It can take children and parents at least a year or more to recover and heal from a divorce. Denial is Ellie's defense against facing and feeling the pain of the divorce. She needs reassurance from both parents that she will be loved and taken care of, even though her parents live apart. As the grieving process continues, Ellie is likely to experience anger, anxiety, and sadness, and eventually come to accept the divorce as a reality. Then she can heal and grow.

Drawing by Ellie, age 9

My Aunt's House

Tina drew a picture of herself at her aunt's house. Later, during her interview alone with me, she told me of her wish to live with her aunt: "She has a pretty house and no children. She's like a mother and she takes me places."

Since her parents' separation, Tina had been living with her father. She had not seen her mother for a year. She said she did not want to see her because she drank too much and because she was afraid her mother would take her away and not bring her back. She appeared to be searching for a "good" mother, one who would not leave her, one who did not drink or make her fearful.

Children need *two* parents they can trust and feel safe with. Grandparents, stepparents, aunts, uncles, and others are also important, but they don't make up for a close relationship with parents.

Parents who have a drug addiction or a drinking problem owe it to themselves and their children to seek help. The other parent should make every effort to help the child, by keeping in close contact or reestablishing contact if necessary. Counseling can be helpful when children do not want to see a parent. Even sporadic visits have been found to be better for a child than no visits at all.

Drawing by Tina, age 9

THE COZY COTTAGE

The cozy cottage Diana drew symbolizes the kind of home most children long for. When parents are willing to cooperate following separation and divorce, children are able to experience having not one but *two* cozy nests.

Shared-parenting arrangements give children the security of having two involved parents in their lives. There are many different kinds of shared-parenting or joint-custody plans. Children can spend equal amounts of time in both homes, or more time during the week with one parent and more weekend and vacation time with the other. (For more information on shared parenting, see Chapter 5, *Joint Custody: Sparing Your Child by Sharing Your Child.*)

Drawing by Diana, age 9

Many children express tremendous love in their drawings, but for some, the love is very sad.

THE SAD KNIGHT

Shawn drew a knight with a sad dog's face and a man's body, legs, and feet. The knight is carrying a bow and arrow. There is a big teardrop falling from each of the sad knight's eyes, and overhead, a broken heart.

Shawn's parents were competing for his love, and each asked him to choose where he wanted to live. Shawn didn't want to hurt either of them, and he wished he could live with both of them.

Children should never be asked where they want to live, as this puts them in a no-win situation. Even when they feel lonely and insecure themselves, parents should never put this kind of pressure on their children. It is both parents' responsibility to create a new life for themselves after divorce, without drawing on their children for support. For parents who need help there is counseling, therapy, and many fine support groups (see Chapter 10, *Where to Find Help*).

Drawing by Shawn, age 7

A Heart Bigger than a House

Mia expressed tremendous love for her mother and father in her drawing. She told me sadly that her parents argued over the telephone and when her father came to pick her up. "It makes me feel bad. I wish they would stop."

Regarding the separation, Mia said, "My daddy left and I didn't see him go. I don't get to see him very much. I'm glad my dad will be taking me to ballet now. I'll get to see him more."

During a mediation session a few hours earlier, Mia's parents had reached an agreement to increase her father's time with Mia. At one point during the session, Mia's mother had suddenly become very angry with me when I talked about the child's need to have a close relationship with both parents. She said furiously, "He has gone out of his way to be disruptive. You don't understand how terrible he is. Why do you think it's important for Mia to see her father more?" Then she broke down and sobbed, "I suppose you would have thought it was important for me to see my father. He raped me from three to seven years old. He was in jail for years. He also raped his stepchildren."

Mia's mother was living in the past, not seeing that her daughter needed a close relationship with her own father, who was *not* abusing Mia. She needed someone to help her sort out her past pain and fears from the present, and to help her focus on Mia's need to have a father.

After she calmed down, I helped her to realize that Mia's father was not like her own father. She reconsidered and agreed that Mia could see her father more often.

Drawing by Mia, age 6

A Heart Is Beautiful

Lisa told me her parents fought a lot but that she believed the fighting would stop once the divorce was final. Unfortunately, that was unlikely to happen. Her father would not settle for less than equal time with his children, and her mother was deeply opposed to this. Lisa said, "Daddy says he loves my mom, but my mom says he lies. I can't pick sides, but she doesn't have to hate him. If I was getting a divorce, I wouldn't hate. I wouldn't hang up."

When asked about how their fighting made her feel, she replied, "I don't feel good. They're grown up but they act like babies. I get stuck in the middle. That's not fair to me. They can't talk, so my mom asks me to tell my dad things. I can't wait until the divorce is over. If that's what will make them happy, then I'll be happy."

I didn't have the heart to tell Lisa that some parents continue fighting forever. It is up to parents to end their conflict. Once the marriage is over, it does *no one* any good to keep rehashing the past. To shift gears from being marriage partners to being parent partners requires parents to focus on the present; on their children's needs and how best to meet them. Parents don't have to like each other to be parent partners. They only have to love their children.

Drawing by Lisa, age 10

Many children express a deep need and longing for peace and harmony in their lives—an end to parental conflict.

PEACE FROG

Debbie drew a big green frog and labeled it, "Peace Frog." Her mother had been accusing Debbie's father of not caring about the children; her father had been telling Debbie that her mother was crazy. Debbie kept longing for peace.

Debbie's parents had not yet learned how to be parent partners. They were stuck in the past, hurting, accusing, blaming, and shaming each other. When parents cannot let the past go, they can't really enjoy the present or the future. One good reason for closing the door on the past is that a brighter, more peaceful present and future are then possible. It also allows the children to experience love and harmony in their lives, and gives them a model for resolving conflict.

Drawing by Debbie, age 14

PEACE AND HARMONY

Brigitte drew a peaceful scene and wrote, "Peace and Harmony."
During her interview with me, she told me how frightened she was
when her parents used to fight. "I was in my room crying. They love
each other, but they don't want to show it."

The peace and harmony that Brigitte is pleading for *is* possible. No matter how difficult and terrible things have been in the
past, parents still have the power to create a better, more peaceful
situation for themselves and their children.

Drawing by Brigitte, age 9

SYMMETRY

Dayton, a sensitive boy involved in a vicious custody battle, made a symmetrical drawing, indicating his need for an orderly, harmonious life.

One way parents can help restore order and symmetry in their lives and in their children's lives is to agree on a suitable parenting plan that meets their children's needs *as soon as possible*. There are many different plans to choose from (see Chapter 5, *Joint Custody: Sparing Your Child by Sharing Your Child*).

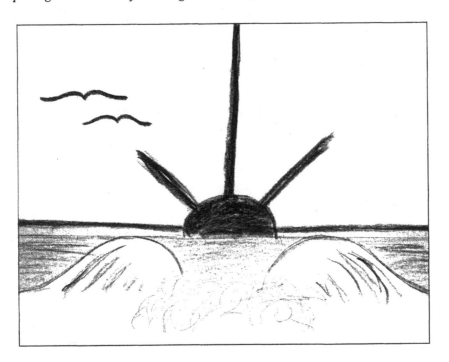

Drawing by Dayton, age 12

Have a Rainbow Day

Betty wishes everyone a "rainbow day," although the raindrops are still falling in her life. This drawing was Betty's way of expressing her deep wish for the storm in her family to pass, and for peace to prevail. A rainbow symbolizes hope, an end to the storm, a return of sunlight and joy, the dawning of a new and brighter day.

Divorcing parents often find it difficult to leave the pain from the marriage behind. There is often a strong desire to blame the other parent for everything and to punish the other parent for causing them pain. This perpetuates the storm, and, in the end, brings no satisfaction for anyone.

A healing affirmation parents might say to themselves is the following: "My children are counting on me. What happened in the past is over. I will learn from my experiences, accept my losses, and create a new beginning for myself and my children."

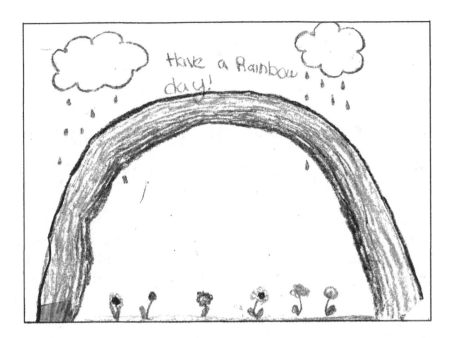

Drawing by Betty, age 10

3

The Power of Mediation: Michael and Other Stories

During my years of mediating child-custody disputes, some parents who have come to me have been open to help; others have rejected it. Some have been so filled with pain and bitterness that they have been unable to go beyond their own problems, but most have been able to work out a viable plan for their children. Here is one story of a difficult mediation that resulted in a successful parenting plan. It is a dramatic example of the power of the mediation process.

Michael, a bright eleven-year-old involved in a custody dispute, was experiencing tremendous pain in spite of the efforts his well-meaning parents made to spare him. The three moving drawings on pages 77–78 reveal Michael's great despair.

Jill and Andrew, Michael's parents, were divorced six years before I first saw them. As happens to many couples, they found themselves in court trying to "win" custody of their son, and were referred for mediation. Their active, bright son was five when his parents divorced, and for a few years after the divorce he lived with his mother in a midwestern state, far away from his father. Then his mother moved back to California, and for the past year he had been living with his father.

During the first session I met with Michael's parents, neither of whom was represented by an attorney. Both were well-educated and held responsible positions. Andrew had remarried; Jill had remained single. They started the session being extremely cordial to each other, but as the session went on they grew tense and frustrated. Each was adamant about having Michael on school days and nights, and each proposed that Michael spend weekends and part of his vacation periods with the other parent. We discussed many alternatives, including various joint-custody arrangements, but neither side was willing to compromise. The only thing both were able to agree on was that Michael was under tremendous stress. Andrew said he has become very concerned about Michael and was taking him to a child psychiatrist. I suggested that I interview Michael alone, and they agreed to bring him the following week.

When I interviewed Michael, it became apparent that he was in deep pain. I asked, "What do you think is going on between your parents?" Michael answered, "First of all they don't talk to each other. They just argue over the phone. My mom says, 'Michael told me he wants to live with me.' Then my dad says, 'That's not what he told me. He told me he wants to live with me.'"

Michael explained that he wasn't telling either of them anything. "I was just listening to them." I asked Michael how that made him feel, and he replied, "Confused. It hurts me when I hear them yelling."

At my request, Michael briefly demonstrated how his mother and father argued, and then said, "It's horrible. I don't know what to do."

I asked if he ever told his parents how upset he felt about their arguments. He said that he had, then added, "I want time to myself. This really gets to me." When I asked how long this arguing has been going on, he replied sadly, "Five years."

I asked how he liked living with his dad and his stepmother. He answered, "Fine. I'm getting good grades."

He said he saw his mother every other weekend and some evenings, but that that wasn't enough time. So I asked him, "Do you have some idea of how you could see your mother more often?" He responded with the following plan: "I could be with one of them on weekdays and one weekend a month, and with the other all the other weekends and for two months in the summer."

When I asked what he thought would happen, he answered, "The way it's going now, it's going to get worse if they don't get help."

In response to my question, "What would you like to see happen now?" Michael answered, "I wouldn't want them to get back together, that wouldn't please me. But I don't want them to fight with each other, and I don't want my mother to give me any more messages or notes for my father."

I asked Michael if he would give me permission to share what we talked about with his parents. Without any hesitation, he said yes.

Michael's parents and stepmother joined us in the room. In Michael's presence, I summarized his interview. Afterward I commented to Michael, "We all understand how upsetting this has been for you. I hope I can help your parents reach an agreement so things can be settled. If they can't reach an agreement here, the judge will have to decide."

After the family conference, I told Michael I wanted to speak to his parents alone. I offered him some crayons and paper. He accepted them and walked down the hall to the waiting room.

I had hoped that hearing Michael's concerns would make a difference and help his parents settle their dispute, but they started immediately to express their deep mistrust of each other. Jill said she resented Andrew's demands. Andrew said he felt unheard, and he stated his position sternly: "I want Michael to have one home." Jill cried and said, "No matter what I do he manipulates. He'd like to see me out of the picture."

I suggested that they consider sharing time with their son more or less equally. It was then that Michael knocked on the door and brought in his drawings to show us. They clearly revealed the pain and pressure he was experiencing.

In one drawing, two heads—labeled "Mom" and "Dad"—faced each other. Out of their mouths Michael had written, "Grrrr." Below them was a small boy labeled "me." From the boy's mouth came the words "Why oh why oh why!"

In another drawing, a boy was being pulled in different directions by two hands, labeled "Mom" and "Dad." The boy's eyes each looked at a different parent. The words "No more" were coming from both sides of the boy's mouth, directed at each parent. Michael told me that the boy was him and that the red streaks coming from his chest were blood from his heart; his hands were also dripping blood.

In the third dynamic picture, he had drawn a large figure of Annie, the character from the musical and movie. She was singing, "The sun'll come out, tomorrow!" Below, a small stick figure labeled "me" was saying, "I like her singing but I wish the words were true."

When Michael left the room again, I expressed my concern for

his well-being. I cautioned his parents about the negative consequences for Michael should their conflict continue. The drawings
had made a great impression on them, and after some discussion
they agreed to return for a third session.

Two weeks later, Jill and Andrew sat in my office again. Jill said
she would agree to joint custody if Andrew would. She wanted the
summers split in half. Andrew said he would be willing to expand
her time with Michael to two months in the summer and overnight
on Wednesday nights, in addition to alternate weekends.

After much discussion they came to a temporary agreement
giving Michael equal time with each parent. They agreed to return
in three months to reevaluate their plan and to discuss a permanent
parenting plan. In the meantime, Andrew said he wanted to discuss
Michael's situation with his son's psychiatrist. I suggested that Jill be
included in those discussions. Both parents agreed.

When Jill and Andrew returned three months later, they were
in agreement about sharing legal and physical custody. They had
attended two conferences with the psychiatrist and one with Mi-

chael's teacher. Both said they wanted to settle things as soon as possible to alleviate stress for Michael, and they were able to work out a parenting plan that allowed Michael to spend two weekdays with Jill, three weekdays with Andrew, and alternate weekends with each parent. They agreed to use the school as a buffer between homes so Michael might experience less tension than if he went directly from one home to another.

The agreement was written up and signed by both parents. Before they left, I asked them what it was that had enabled them to reach the agreement. Jill said, "I feel less threatened now, which helped me to be able to try out a shared-parenting arrangement. I see it can work. I also think Andrew and his wife feel a little more trust in me now." Andrew remarked, "I feel less threatened as well. I think Jill understands that I have my own life. I was concerned that she would try to interfere." Jill and Andrew agreed to return to conciliation court to reevaluate their parenting plan before the next school year began.

Child-custody mediation gave Michael's parents, stepmother, and Michael the opportunity to communicate their feelings, concerns, and needs. It also helped Michael's parents focus more on Michael's needs and on the present and future instead of on the past. The temporary agreement helped them to build trust as parents and to begin to develop a cooperative parenting relationship. Without mediation, Michael's parents could have gone on torturing their son for many more years. Instead, in time, Michael may come to believe little Annie's words: that "the sun'll come out tomorrow" after all.

Avoid Recycling Pain and Blame from the Past

Past resentments related to the marriage—such as who caused the separation and divorce; who left the other and why; feelings such as hurt and anger regarding the other man or woman in the picture; disappointment; helplessness; the desire to reconcile—have nothing to do with the children and should be dealt with separately.

Nora was a distraught young mother with two girls, seven and nine years old. She told me bluntly that she would never let them see their father. Crying, she went on to say that their father had left her and the children for another woman, that he was not to be trusted, and that she had told her girls "the truth" about their father.

I explained to Nora that what she was doing was harming her daughters and making them mistrust men, which would cause them terrible problems later on. She answered me bitterly, "Good. I want them to mistrust men, so they won't get hurt the way I have."

When parents mix past marriage issues with present parenting issues, they cause problems for their children and get little satisfaction themselves. For your child's sake, in your dealings with the other parent stick to issues concerning your child, such as what your child needs, who will supply those needs, special problems, parents' and children's schedules, medical appointments, classes, recreational activities, and future plans.

The four-step process below can assist parents in shifting gears and leaving past resentments behind.

1. Seek out and acknowledge your role, the part *you* played in creating at least some of the problems you have had, or are having, with the other parent.

2. Accept responsibility for what you did without blaming yourself or the other parent.

3. Formulate a plan for correcting and improving the situation through changes in your own attitudes and behavior.

4. Carry out your plan patiently, and avoid falling back into old patterns.

Once parents are able to accept the fact that they share responsibility, there is no longer a need to blame each other, and real headway can be made toward establishing a workable parental relationship. This is exactly what children need to feel loved and secure.

Minimize the Pain for Children

Ted, a young father of a four-year-old boy, was seeing his son every other weekend. He told me with tears in his eyes, "I think it would be best if I stopped seeing Adam. He cries when I take him back to his mother's. He clings to me and won't let me go. It breaks me up. I can't stand it."

I explained that it is natural for children not to want to leave a parent, especially when they don't see that parent very often. I suggested that, as painful as it might be for him, he should try to see Adam more often and reassure him that they will be seeing each other soon again. I explained that most children gradually get used to the separations, and added, "It takes time. Ted, if you really want to break Adam's heart, stop seeing him. He'll never get over that one."

Many parents who become estranged from their children are literally squeezed out by a short-sighted, hostile other parent who wants to get even or who is threatened and unwilling to share. These parents can't help the way they feel, but they can help what they do. When they allow their emotions to rule them, they shortchange their children for life.

Prolonged parental conflict seriously undermines children's security and trust in their parents, in themselves, and in their futures. Their deep mistrust, in turn, keeps them from experiencing happiness and satisfaction in their own lives—as children and when they grow up.

It is essential that parents get off to a good start following a separation, or at least very soon thereafter. They should make every effort to correct a bad situation. If not, they will find themselves in a terrible nightmare, causing endless misery for themselves and their children.

———

Mediation is a powerful process. It is an alternative that is humane, highly effective, and appropriate for most child-custody or visitation disputes. It pays for parents to give divorce mediation a try when they are unable to settle their problems and differences. The courtroom process should be resorted to only when all else fails.

4

Creating a Conflict-Free Zone for Your Child

If children are to succeed after divorce, they must be protected from parental conflict and allowed to enjoy close relationships with both parents. Despite pain, resentment, and disagreements, it is possible for divorced parents to surround their children with a "conflict-free" zone.

The diagram below shows a child in a small circle, the conflict-free zone. It is surrounded by a larger circle, the parental conflict zone. The space between the two circles is a buffer zone between the child and the parental conflict.

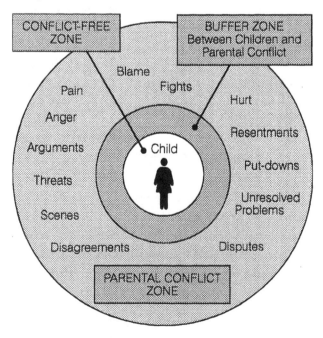

The buffer zone is a neutral area. In this conflict-free zone, the child is shielded from the put-downs, arguments, threats, and tension that accompany disagreements.

To create a conflict-free zone, parents must learn to control and restrain themselves. They must have the consideration to refrain from arguing and fighting when their child is present. They should save discussion of volatile issues for a time when their child is not around. It is easy for one embittered ex-partner to glare at the other or to make a sarcastic remark. One thing leads to another, and before long the children are witnessing another argument. And they never witness it as detached observers. Because most children are attached to *both* parents, each unkind remark is like a physical blow. Aside from frightening them and making them miserable, such episodes teach children negative lessons about life and about relationships. The images will remain with them forever.

It is hard enough to raise a child right under the best of circumstances, when the parents are living together and getting along. It is much more difficult to raise a child when the parents are separated and having difficulty getting along. It takes special thought, effort, and courage for divorcing parents to provide their children with a safe environment that enables them to grow up feeling good about their lives and about themselves.

It is natural to want to blame the other parent and to feel like a victim; real honesty and courage are required to realize that we are *each* responsible for what happens to us. The choice to enter into the relationship was ours. The course of the relationship was determined by what we did. Had we done things differently, the relationship and outcome might have been different. Once we can accept that we were part of what caused the breakdown, we feel more in charge of our lives and less like victims.

Taking responsibility for what happens to us is very difficult— but it is essential. If one spouse physically or verbally abuses the other, and the abused spouse accepts that behavior, that spouse also has a responsibility for allowing the situation to continue. No one wants to be mistreated, but people tend to seek and find a relationship that suits their needs. Much of how we are treated by others depends on how we feel about ourselves. If we feel worthy of respect and love, we are more likely to choose a positive and loving situation. We learn and grow when we stop blaming others and begin to observe and change our behavior and attitudes.

A Code of Conduct for Parent Partners

Below are ten guidelines that may help you establish a conflict-free zone. These suggestions are a code of conduct, a positive guide on how to treat the other parent. If you follow them, your child will be much less likely to be caught in the crossfire of continual parental conflict.

Each suggestion touches on a different aspect of the parental relationship. The first suggestion lays the groundwork for establishing a parental relationship after separation or divorce. The second and sixth suggestions are about the need to respect the other parent's rights to privacy and to private time with the child. The third, fourth, and fifth call on parents to avoid critical and hostile interactions. The last four suggestions encourage trust and cooperation and assist in developing positive problem-solving skills.

If at times following these guidelines is difficult, remember this: when you treat the other parent with respect, you are doing it for your child and for yourself, *not* for the other parent.

1. Shift gears from being marriage partners to being parent partners.

During a marriage, parents take on the roles of "husband-wife" as well as "mother-father." The diagram below shows that after a divorce they remain only "mother-father," or "parent partners."

Making the change from a husband-wife relationship to a solely mother-father relationship may be difficult. It requires focusing on the present and on your child's needs, not on your resentments and regrets. The first step is to stop blaming the other parent and to begin to examine and acknowledge your share of the responsibility for the breakdown of the marriage.

The outcome of any marriage is determined by both spouses, not just one. Each person's attitudes and behaviors affect their rela-

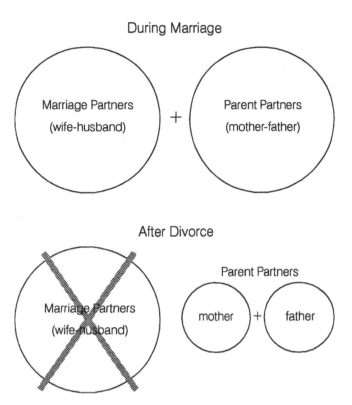

During Marriage

Marriage Partners (wife-husband) + Parent Partners (mother-father)

After Divorce

Marriage Partners (wife-husband)

Parent Partners

mother + father

tionship for better or worse, and ultimately affect the quality of their own life. People who insist on blaming their spouse for the breakup of their marriage tend to see themselves as helpless, as victims. Sadly, they also tend to remain weak, depressed, and bitter long after the divorce. Some never recover. In contrast people who are willing to accept some responsibility for the divorce tend to learn from the past, experience new personal growth, and eventually feel healed.

2. Settle disagreements through give-and-take and compromise, and respect individual differences.

It is difficult to give in, especially when you feel hurt, threatened, or controlled. So when the other parent asks you for a favor or change of schedule, it may seem satisfying to say no. Chances are that the next time you want something changed or rearranged, you will also get no for an answer. Small disagreements escalate into bigger ones, and in this struggle the one who gets hurt is your child.

I strongly recommend that you say yes to the other parent whenever you can, and compromise whenever possible. This does not mean you should allow yourself to be taken advantage of; it means you should be flexible.

Ron and Sharon shared the parenting of their two children. Ron called Sharon to ask if he could keep the children an extra day to attend a special family gathering. Sharon said, "No, it's not your day," and slammed down the receiver. People usually find a way to get even, and Ron did. When Sharon asked Ron to change the schedule so she could take the children to her company picnic, Ron refused.

Ron and Sharon's struggle caused the children to miss *two* important occasions and created many hard feelings between the parents. It would have been far better for them to have given a little extra consideration to each other, thus heading off frustration and pain for their children and themselves.

To prevent constant hassles and arguments, it is essential that parents learn to avoid power struggles and to respect the differences between them. They can learn to recognize and avoid fighting over issues that parents often argue about, such as differences in lifestyle, religious beliefs, and values; the children's proper bedtime; what foods the children should eat; how often they should be bathed; what recreation and sports they should be offered; whether their teeth need to be straightened; and which doctor to use.

Two parents I counseled were in a dispute over their children's religious education. Linda wanted the children to attend Sunday school, but Ed did not believe in organized religion. Ed said he refused to be "a phony" by telling the children he believed in their religion when he didn't, despite Linda's expectation that he do so.

I explained to Linda and Ed that it is common for two parents—even husbands and wives—to feel differently on a number of issues, including religion. Each parent has a unique point of view and the right to share it with his or her children. When there are differences of opinion, parents should tell their children, "Daddy and I (or Mommy and I) see things differently." Then each parent can tell them what he or she believes without belittling the other parent's point of view.

In this case, Linda had the right to send her children to Sunday school if she wanted to when the children were with her, and Ed had the right not to send them.

When parents continually argue, their children get caught in the middle. They worry constantly about having to take sides and about pleasing both parents. Children should understand that it is natural for people to have differing points of view. As they grow up, they will have their own way of seeing things. It is important for parents to teach respect for individual differences.

3. Treat the other parent with respect, and avoid making derogatory statements about the other parent in the presence of your child.

You don't have to like the other parent to say hello when he or she calls or comes to pick up the children. You would probably show a stranger that much respect. When you treat the other parent in a civil, cordial manner, it helps create a more harmonious environment for you and your children.

During an interview with a ten-year-old boy, I asked how he was getting along with his father. The boy hesitated, so I asked, "Is there some problem you're having with your dad?"

He replied, "My dad always says bad things about my mom. He says she isn't a good mom. The things he says about her are not true."

I asked, "How does that make you feel about your dad?"

He answered angrily, "I don't like it. I ask him to stop but he keeps on doing it."

Children need to look up to both parents. When one parent treats the other badly or makes derogatory remarks to the children about him or her, children are forced to take sides. This causes them to feel extremely uncomfortable and pressured, the opposite of what they need to feel good about themselves and to succeed.

4. Avoid arguments, scenes, threats, fights, and violence, especially when your children are present.

Children tell me how frightened and helpless they feel when their parents argue or fight. No matter how upset the adults are, how angry they feel, and how much they feel like hurting the other parent for causing them pain, for their children's sake they *must* avoid threats, violence, and confrontations in front of their children.

Twelve-year-old Marc told me sadly, "My dad came over and ruined my birthday. He called my mom names and accused her of untrue things. My dad drinks a lot. I wish he'd stop drinking and get help for himself. I'm really mad at him."

Threats and violence can lead to terrible problems for children and parents alike. Ron, a young father of a two-year-old son, found it hard even to talk to me. He sat for a while with his head in his hands. Then he began to speak, "It was terrible. Sue forced me to leave the house. I was having so many pressures. I pleaded with her to take me back, but she wouldn't." The next day Ron pushed his way into the house against Sue's wishes and refused to leave. He grabbed her and shook her to try to make her understand his feelings. A neighbor called the police, who came and escorted Ron out. Ron went home and telephoned Sue. "I told her I was coming to kill her. I really didn't mean it." This time the police arrested Ron on the basis of a complaint Sue made.

While Ron waited outside my office, Sue told me her side. There had been previous incidents of violence, and she had gone to court to get a restraining order to force Ron to leave the house. When he pushed his way in and refused to leave, she tried to get out but he wouldn't let her go. He grabbed her, and she screamed. A neighbor called the police. Their son watched the whole incident. Sue said tearfully, "Later that day Ron threatened to kill both me and our son. I'm afraid to let our son go with Ron alone unless he gets some help for himself."

Because of the threats and violence, Sue had initiated a case to limit Ron's visitation rights. By the time I saw them, Sue wasn't willing to settle things. She wanted the judge to order monitored visitation for Ron, so he could visit his son only in the presence of a third party. Ron wasn't willing to agree, and the battle continued.

The ones who suffer most in this kind of situation are the children. Sometimes, as a result of threats or violence, the frightened parent moves far away, and the children lose a parent in the process. Parents who are genuinely concerned about their children's well-being will avoid confrontations in front of the children. They can discuss sensitive issues over the telephone or at private meetings out of the presence of their children, or by mail. To avoid conflict, child-support payments should be sent by mail, not given when picking up or returning the children.

The wish of almost every child I interview is that their parents not argue or fight. Only parents can grant this wish. I suggest that parents experience their hurt and anger without acting them out, and especially not in front of their children. Parents who find they cannot control their anger owe it to themselves and their offspring to seek help.

5. Don't be overly critical of or try to control the other parent.

Unless your child is really in danger while with the other parent, it is advisable not to be picky, critical, or too demanding. Let small concerns or irritations pass. If the other parent is a few minutes late once in a while, it is better not to make a fuss. Instead, discuss major issues that concern your rights or your child's health, safety, education, and welfare.

The way you tell the other parent about your concerns will make a difference in the way she or he responds to you. If you demand, attack, blame, or threaten, you will get a defensive response. Threatening statements, such as, "If you ever take my children to your girlfriend's house, I'll never let you take them again," or, "If you are even five minutes late, I'll be gone and you'll just have to miss seeing the children this week," will only anger the other person—and provoke him or her to retaliate.

Even when you feel annoyed and furious with the other parent, keep the peace for your children's sake. State your complaints in a

positive manner without being abusive, sarcastic, or overly demanding. If, for example, you are upset or inconvenienced by some behavior of the other parent, or if there is something special you wish
to communicate to him or her, say what you need to without being
defensive or bringing up the past. If you can't control yourself in
person, write a cordial note.

Phrase your concerns in a positive way. For example: "I begin
to worry when you are more than a half hour late returning Johnny.
Please give me a call if you're running late. I would really appreciate
this." Or, "Please put in an extra change of clothes and a warm
jacket this week. We're planning to go camping, and I want to be
sure Dana stays dry and warm." Or, "Please remember to give Lisa
her medicine. Dr. Henry said she should have it four times a day.
The directions are on the bottle. Thanks."

6. Avoid pressuring the other parent about getting back together, and respect the other parent's privacy.

Trying to persuade the other parent to reconcile when he or she
does not want to will not only cause problems for your child but also
increase your feelings of frustration and rejection. If your former
husband or wife wanted to be with you again, he or she would find
a way for you to be together.

After their separation, Ned telephoned Dianne at work almost
daily, and sometimes several times a day, to talk to her about getting
back together. Ned also insisted on discussing the possibility of reconciliation every time he came to pick up Andrew, their four-year-
old son. There had been frequent arguments and even a few violent
scenes in front of the child. Dianne had made it very clear to Ned
that the marriage was over, but he was persistent and would become
so upset when she wasn't seeing things his way that he would become abusive. He had hit Dianne a number of times in the past, and
now threatened that if Dianne were ever to bring another man near
his son, he might not be able to control himself.

Dianne felt she had to do something to protect herself and
Andrew, so she moved two thousand miles away. Ned lost not only
Dianne, but his son as well. Now he sees Andrew only a few weeks

each year, a situation that he helped to create, and a tremendous loss for both father and son.

Ned can't be blamed for feeling devastated by the end of his marriage, but he could have controlled what he said to Dianne and the way he behaved toward her. Dianne had a right to her own life and her privacy. Ned would have been far better off if he had sought the services of a professional counselor, psychologist, or psychiatrist for support and help in getting through this difficult time.

7. Don't sacrifice your child over money.

Some parents refuse to agree to anything until all the financial issues are settled, but financial settlements can take years. In the meantime, children should not be left hanging in the balance. As soon as the separation occurs, parents should cooperate in making suitable and appropriate arrangements so that their children can have time with both parents.

Disputes over which parent will keep the house can be agonizing for children. Sharon and Ian continued to live in the same home because neither was willing to leave. This led to constant quarrels, which their two children witnessed daily. They also fought daily over who would have the children each day. It was almost two years before the financial situation was settled. In the meantime, the children were tormented by their parents' lack of sensitivity, respect, and cooperation. Their six-year-old daughter Amy told me, "Some days I can't say hello to my daddy, because my mommy says it is not his day. When it's my daddy's day, I can't say hello to my mommy."

The situation was perhaps even worse for Carl and Juanita's two teenage children. The parents were so busy battling over the financial issues that neither of them was willing to make a home for their children. Juanita was living with her mother. She told me, "There's no room for the children there. When I get some money, I'll get my own place and take them." Carl lived in a bachelor apartment where they didn't allow children. He said, "If Juanita will agree to the financial settlement, I'll get a bigger apartment and take the children." Each blamed the other for delays in settling the financial situation, and each wanted the other to take responsibility for their children.

Juanita sent their daughter Carla to a boarding school, and Carla couldn't come home on weekends because both her parents demanded that the other parent keep her.

Juanita put their son Gary and all his belongings outside her door one day and called Carl to come and pick him up. Carl came to get him, but since no children were allowed to live in his building, Gary had to sneak in the back way. His parents told me that Gary threatened suicide several times during the next few months.

Long after such situations occur, scars will remain. No matter how upset and frustrated parents are over unresolved financial issues, they should respect their child's right to see both parents under a workable, peaceable arrangement.

8. Make child-support payments on time.

Child support is an important parental responsibility. The purpose of child support is to try to equalize the quality of life for children in both homes. Making child-support payments on time will help avoid arguments between you and the other parent and will help keep your child's life running smoothly.

Children should not be burdened with support problems or be made to ask for it. When parents cannot come to an agreement about child support, they should let the court decide the issue. Once a decision has been made, child-support payments should be paid regularly and promptly. If a parent refuses to pay, the other parent can call on the district attorney's office for assistance.

As important as child-support payments are, children should not be kept from seeing a parent because a payment has not been made. Money issues and parent-child relationship issues are separate and should be kept separate. Otherwise, children not only lose financial support but also valuable and needed time with a parent—a double punishment.

One small boy told me, "I can't see my daddy because he doesn't pay child support. If he loved me, he would pay."

If this child is not helped to feel loved, he may grow into an adult with low self-esteem and have little chance of being happy and successful. His father will be partly responsible because he did not send child-support payments on time; his mother will be partly responsible because she mixed money issues with visitation issues. Unfortunately, their son will have paid the price for their uncooperative behavior.

9. Gain the other parent's trust by keeping your agreements and promises.

Rebuilding trust between divorced parents is essential. It helps them create the conflict-free zone in which their children can thrive. When agreements are not kept, anger, disappointment, hostility, resentment, grudges, and retaliation follow. Before long the situation becomes terrible for the children, as in the cases described below.

After Bob returned the children hours late on Mother's Day, Leslie retaliated by refusing to give Bob the children at all on Father's Day. They were in court two months later.

When Fran was not home at the agreed-upon time to receive the children, Roy waited around for half an hour, then left with the children. Later that evening, an argument ensued over the telephone. Their children overheard and were scared.

A mother of a two-year-old told me, "I can't trust Mike. He gets busy doing stuff and he doesn't watch Scott. Scott got hurt twice when he was at his dad's place. Mike leaves his tools around, and Scott could hurt himself on the saws. And Mike doesn't always use the car seat."

A father of a nine-year-old told me worriedly, "Lisa left my son asleep and went to the store. What if a fire had broken out?"

The best way to build trust is by being a responsible parent. This means caring for your child in a safe and responsible way. Babies and young children need the constant supervision and protection of an adult. Older children and adolescents need parental supervision appropriate to their age.

10. Accept the facts that the other parent has the right to spend time with the children, and that your children have the right to a relationship with the other parent.

If you can accept this, it will relieve your children of a great burden, and they will then be free to have a relationship with the other parent. Many children suffer greatly when deprived by divorce of the presence of one parent. If they also lose their relationship with that parent, they will be even more miserable, because they are not being allowed to recover and heal.

Yvonne and Paul had been divorced seven years. Their children, Karen, age fifteen, and Eric, eleven, lived with Yvonne and saw Paul whenever Yvonne would let them.

Paul wanted custody of both children. Eric wanted to live with him. Paul told me, "Yvonne grounds my kids and won't let them see me or talk to me on the phone. I have always supported them, but she has turned them against me."

Yvonne wanted to continue to have custody. "I believe in disciplining my kids," she said. "I took away their privilege to see their father as a punishment for a few months. Then a counselor told me I couldn't do that. She said I should take other privileges away from them. They didn't complain about not seeing their father. They weren't anxious to go. My whole life is those kids." Tears came to her eyes as she spoke. "My main concern is for Paul to stop badgering the kids to live with him and stop talking against me to them."

Paul acknowledged that during the last few months he had been trying to persuade the children to live with him, but he assured me he had made a vow not to do it anymore.

I asked their daughter, Karen, if she remembered when her parents had separated. She replied, "I remember my dad packing and leaving, and him visiting. I remember crying and telling him not to go, but I got over it."

Karen said she had been seeing her father about once a month, which was often enough because of her many activities. How did she feel about being pressured to live with her father, I asked. She said, "I don't know what to say after he asks that. A couple of times I said yes, but most of the time I didn't say anything. It made me feel uncomfortable. I wish everything would calm down and settle out."

Their son, Eric, told me, "My parents are always fighting. My mom aggravates my dad. When we are grounded we can't see my dad, but we can go to the movies. That's not fair to my dad. I want to live with him. I really want to."

"Did you tell your mother?" I asked.

Eric replied, "I told her and she said, 'I don't ever want to see you again.' Later she told my dad to send me home. I want to live with my dad and see my mom some weekends."

Eric's indignation toward his mother and his resentment of her refusal to respect his father's right to see him is fairly common. Once children are old and wise enough to understand and protest against unfair parental attitudes and practices, they rebel. Many of these children want to leave the "unfair" parent to live with the other.

For such children, the loss, and the continuing conflicts are tremendous. Moreover, people who are miserable as children tend to reenact their unresolved conflicts in adulthood. None of this sadness and tragedy need happen, if parents are willing to work together cooperatively.

Cooperate in Raising the Children

Helping your child through your divorce requires cooperation between you and the other parent. Cooperation means:

- settling on a workable parenting plan that gives children access to both parents

- keeping ongoing contact with the children so they don't feel rejected or abandoned

- preparing the children beforehand for the separation, if possible

- reassuring children that they can still count on both parents

- taking the parenting plan seriously

- never disappointing the children at the last minute

- rarely canceling plans with the children

- establishing two homes for the children with a place for their clothes, toys, and other possessions

- maintaining telephone contact with the children

- providing the children telephone access to both parents

- having the children ready on time for the other parent

- receiving the children on time

- calling the other parent when delays are unavoidable

- setting up a "hot line" between parents for discussion of serious problems concerning the children

Cooperation creates an environment in which children feel safe, satisfied, and loved. Cooperation does *not* mean:

- pumping children for information about the other parent

- trying to control the other parent

- using the children to carry angry messages back and forth

- using the children as pawns to hurt the other parent

- using the children to ask for or to deliver child-support payments

- arguing in front of the children

- speaking derogatorily about the other parent in the children's presence

- asking the children with whom they want to live

- putting the children in the position of having to take sides

Parents who choose to cooperate and work together on raising their children after divorce experience many advantages, including:

- fewer problems for the children

- more personal satisfaction and less frustration for the parents

- fewer visitation problems

- fewer child-support problems

- reduced possibility of returning to court

- easier sharing of responsibility

- better parent-child relationships

- more freedom from conflict

- fewer health, emotional, school, and social problems

During the chaotic and emotional period of separation and divorce, parents may think it impossible to cooperate with each other. It is a period of great pain, involving feelings of guilt and failure; the loss of security, friendship, and love; and the necessity of facing some of the less-attractive aspects of oneself such as revenge, bitterness, and great anger. For many, it is the hardest time of their lives.

One parent told me that, looking back, what had freed her from the vicious cycle of guilt, pain, and anger that overwhelmed her after her divorce was putting her children first and putting their needs before her own. In the long term, the ability to deal with her ex-spouse in a controlled way *because she was thinking of someone else* gradually restored her self-esteem and allowed her to heal herself.

Individually and as a society, we must find ways to encourage divorcing parents to think of the future—their children's future, and their own.

5

Joint Custody: Sparing Your Child by Sharing Your Child

For some parents, sharing parenthood with the former partner is a sensitive and painful thing to do. Yet sharing a child is one of the best ways parents can show their love for their child.

A possessive attitude often stems from a parent feeling threatened that he or she will be controlled by the other parent or will lose the child. Many parents cannot imagine how they could get along with a former partner after a divorce when they couldn't get along during the marriage. In her book *Mom's House, Dad's House*, Dr. Isolina Ricci points out that parents do not *have* to be friends or even like the other parent to work together cooperatively regarding their children. They can develop a working relationship similar to the relationship between business partners.

Parenting plan options range all the way from one parent having sole or primary custody and most of the responsibility to both parents having joint custody and sharing the responsibility more or less equally. Whatever the particulars are, a suitable parenting plan should have the children's best interests and needs in mind, as well as the parents' needs, preferences, and schedules. The following factors should be considered when making a plan:

1. The plan should allow both parents to have significant amounts of time with the children.

2. Infants and young children should see and spend time with both parents frequently.

3. School-age children and adolescents should be able to attend school and take part in activities regularly.

4. Parents' work schedules must be accommodated.

5. Some flexibility should be incorporated and provision should be made for making changes.

6. The plan should be reevaluated periodically in terms of the children's progress and modified, if necessary, to meet their changing needs.

Consider Shared Parenting or Joint Custody

Some parents believe that if they have sole custody, they won't ever have to deal with the other parent again. In reality, they will have to deal with the other parent as long as they and their children are alive. Other parents believe that joint custody means that their child must live with one parent for six months, then with the other parent for six months, changing schools every semester. Most parents—with good reason—are against that idea.

There are two terms you need to know pertaining to joint custody: *joint-legal* and *joint-physical*. In practice, *joint-legal custody* means that both parents have the right to make major decisions about their children's health, education, and welfare. If a serious problem about your children arises, you would probably both want to discuss it and make these decisions together anyway. Joint-legal custody does not mean you can control each other or that one of you can tell the other how to live. With joint-legal custody, each of you still has a separate relationship with your children. This means that when you are with your children, you are in charge.

Joint-physical custody means that children will live with each of you for specified amounts of time according to a plan that you develop. That plan should consider factors such as the children's ages, school schedules, and activity schedules. It must also consider parents' work schedules and availability. Parents should be sensitive to how the children respond to their plan.

For many women, one serious concern about shared parenting is financial. They worry that if they give the children to the father half of the time, they will not get child support. If a woman earns as much as a man does, this may be true; however, if he earns substantially more than she does, he would ordinarily be asked to contribute more than she does toward the children's support. The deciding issue here is whether he has the ability to pay more than she does, not whether he has the children half the time.

Parents and children have much to gain from shared parenting. First of all, it is natural for each parent to continue to have responsibility for raising a child after divorce.

A second advantage is that sharing custody encourages both parents to remain involved in their children's lives and to assume parental duties and responsibilities. This is an important advantage when one considers the fact that approximately one-third of the children of divorce completely lose contact with one of their parents.

A third advantage is that shared-custody arrangements meet children's needs. Children tend to progress well and feel better about themselves when they have close and continuous contact with both parents.

Shared-custody arrangements meet parental needs too. Joint-custody parents have the same rights and shared responsibilities; this avoids one parent becoming overburdened and burned out from trying to do everything alone. In shared-custody arrangements, each parent has significant amounts of time with the children and time without the children. This enables them to maintain close relationships with their children, as well as build a new life and other relationships for themselves.

Shared custody equalizes the balance of power between parents. Parents who share custody tend to feel less threatened about losing their children than a noncustodial parent would. This balance of power is likely to reduce power struggles, the need to compete, litigation, and tugging back and forth on the children, and will generate an all-around better outcome for the children.

False Assumptions About Joint Custody

The main arguments raised by parents and some professionals against joint custody are the following:

1. Children need the stability of one home. Going back and forth is too hard and disruptive on children.

2. Mothers are more suited to caring for children than fathers.

3. Divorcing parents cannot get along well enough to share custody.

4. Joint custody will lead to more hassles, arguments, and litigation.

These arguments were repudiated in a research study done at the Philadelphia Child Guidance Clinic (see *References,* 1). Of the forty-three families studied by Deborah Ann Leupnitz, Ph.D., 55 percent of the single-custody parents returned to court at least once over money or visitation issues, while none of the joint-custody parents did so in spite of disagreements. Dr. Leupnitz's study also showed that joint-custody fathers supported their children reliably, that children whose parents shared custody were pleased and comfortable with the arrangement, and that joint-custody parents did not feel as overwhelmed by the pressure of raising a child alone as the single-custody parents did. Another study compared litigation following sole-custody awards with joint-custody awards showed significantly less litigation following joint-custody awards even when parents were ordered to have joint custody against their will (see *References,* 2).

In my opinion, security for a child is based on close and loving relationships with both parents and not necessarily on having only one home. In matters of comfort and lifestyle, children are adaptive and resilient. They can adjust to many changes and schedules as long as they are not fought over continually and not deprived of their parents. In the United States, most mothers work and less than 13 percent stay home with their children. From an early age, children are bundled up and taken to baby-sitters, where they spend most of their waking hours. Yet many of these working mothers object to having the children spend time at the father's home because, they say, it would be too disruptive. This is inconsistent and self-serving. Fathers can be nurturing parents too. The liberation of women has freed men to become more involved fathers.

It is a positive sign that more and more fathers are asking for joint custody and more meaningful involvement in their children's lives. Children need *two* involved parents. After divorce, parents *can* learn how to get along and share parenting responsibilities, even if they were not able to get along as husband and wife.

Historically, child custody has now come full circle. Until about one hundred years ago, fathers usually got custody of the children, because at that time fathers were at home, working their farms. Once men began to work in factories and mothers remained at home, mothers were traditionally awarded custody, unless they were deemed unfit to raise the children. The pendulum is beginning to swing back to center toward both parents sharing custody, and toward both parents continuing to raise the children after divorce.

Work Out a Suitable Parenting Plan

No matter what form of custody arrangement you desire or choose, it is critical that you and the other parent work out a suitable parenting plan as soon as possible. Following are some suggestions for shared physical-custody plans and shared-parenting plans.

When parents live fairly close, they can share physical custody in a number of ways. Their children can spend alternate weekends and two days each week with each parent, or half of the week with each, or full weeks on an alternating basis. For younger children, frequent access to both parents is important, since a whole week is a long time for a young child. For school-age children, alternate weeks with each parent, or more time with one parent during weekdays and more weekend and vacation time with the other, are appropriate. In planning for adolescents, schedules should be flexible enough to accommodate their activities.

When parents live far apart, the children can spend the school year with one parent and most of their vacation time with the other parent, alternating every two or three years. Rotating too often might disrupt a child's education and activities.

Parents can be as creative as they like in developing a shared-parenting plan, as long as the plan has the children's needs in mind. Children should be monitored closely to see that they are doing well with the plan parents have selected. Changes in schedules may be needed as situations and needs change. It is important that the spirit of joint custody remains: that parents share rights and responsibilities and that the children have two homes. Parents usually share driving children to school and activities, and children have clothes, toys, and friends in both homes.

A suitable parenting arrangement can give you and your children much-needed structure and security. It will help your children feel less confused and less worried about losing you or the other parent. Once a workable parenting arrangement is agreed upon, or ordered by the court, it should be taken seriously. Only in case of real emergency should it be canceled, although changes can be made by mutual agreement between parents.

Special Considerations for Infants and Young Children

Infants and very young children need frequent access to both parents. An arrangement that allows the infant or young child to spend time with the other parent often, such as every few days, is preferable to plans that allow contact only weekly or twice a month.

When an infant or young child does not know or remember one parent, every effort should be made to help the child develop a close relationship with that parent. The first few visits should be brief and spaced fairly close together, preferably with a mutually agreed-upon third person present whom the child knows. This requires cooperation on the part of both parents, patience, and a certain amount of inconvenience; however, it is less traumatic for the infant or young child than a longer meeting with only a stranger. As the child becomes familiar and comfortable with the parent, the length of the visits can gradually be increased.

Rita and Ron's eight-month-old baby was just three months old when they separated. Ron was rarely allowed to see his son and then only in Rita's presence. He told me angrily, "He's my son, too. I have as much right to him as she does. I want him every other weekend."

Rita responded, "He's too young. You never took care of him; you were always out drinking with your friends. You're only interested in him now because your mother wants to see him." She looked at Ron with tremendous anger.

I asked Rita, "What are you most angry at Ron for?"

She burst into tears. "Ron wants to take my baby. I'm still nursing him. Maybe when he's older. Ron doesn't know how to take care of him."

I hear this story often from mothers of infants. In part, their difficulty with letting go has to do with the symbiotic tie that exists between an infant and mother from the time when the baby was in the womb, a bond that is both physical and psychological. This tie causes mother and infant to feel as one unit, bonded together. Nursing mothers and their infants are especially tied to each other. Fortunately, now that many fathers are involved in the birthing process and in caring for their infants right from birth, fathers can also experience a close bonding with their infants.

Difficult as it may be for a mother to let go of her infant, it is essential that a baby spend time with the father also. The father should be given written instructions regarding feeding and care. Short periods away from the mother can gradually be extended as the child grows. During times when the mother is working or is otherwise unavailable to take care of her child, the father should be given first right to provide care if he can do so. Time together helps the father and infant develop the close relationship the child needs. Children are happiest and liveliest when both parents are involved in their lives, and when they feel close to and comfortable with both parents.

Arrangements for School-age Children

School-age children benefit from longer periods with each parent, including spending some nights in the father's as well as the mother's home. Children of this age need to be encouraged to love both parents and also stepparents, grandparents, and relatives from both sides of the family. Parenting arrangements should allow them to participate in social, sports, and recreational activities connected with their school. Ideally, both parents should be involved in their children's education and should encourage them to do homework assignments. In each home, the child should have a place to study and an atmosphere in which he or she can be free from commotion and television. Children should be taken to school on time, and should not miss school except for illness or other important reasons.

Arrangements for Adolescents

Adolescents need to be allowed to pursue their own interests and social relationships. They should not be expected to stay home and hold Mom's or Dad's hand. They need freedom from overwhelming responsibility for major family decisions. They need parents who act like parents, not like pals; parents who do not constantly lean on them for moral support; cooperative parents who do not pressure them to take sides. Because they are not yet mature, they also need ongoing contact with both parents and continued guidance about rules and standards for their behavior. At the same time, they need privacy, activities with other adolescents, and some flexibility concerning schedules. Admittedly, working around an adolescent's schedule can be frustrating, but parents must make the effort.

Cindy, age fifteen, told me, "My problem is that I play in a girl's softball league and sometimes we have games or practices when I'm supposed to be with my dad. My dad gets upset. He says he only gets to see me every other weekend and it ruins his plans. He blames my mom for letting me sign up for the league. It's not her fault. I wanted to play."

It is natural for adolescents to want to be involved in activities, and it is hard for them to keep their parents happy and still satisfy themselves. There are no simple solutions. Occasionally, the adolescent could compromise by missing a practice or event; at other times, parents could change their schedules to accommodate the adolescent's plans. Even though parental rights to see the child should be respected, some flexibility is essential.

Avoid Holiday Hassles

The holiday season can be an especially lonely time for single parents without their children. When there are hassles over schedules, no one enjoys the holidays. However, with some forethought and planning, you can create enjoyable holiday arrangements. Since Christmas is often a sensitive holiday, I will use it as an example.

Here are several ways parents can work out the Christmas holiday:

1. Children could spend Christmas Eve through Christmas morning at 9:00 or 10:00 A.M. with one parent; Christmas Day through December 26 at 9:00 or 10:00 A.M. with the other; then reverse this order the following year.

2. Children could spend the entire Christmas holiday with one parent one year and with the other parent the following year.

3. Children could spend Christmas morning with one parent and Christmas afternoon with the other and reverse this the following year.

4. Children could spend Christmas Eve with one parent and Christmas Day with the other every year, if parents prefer this because of family traditions.

5. Parents could spend the holidays together with the children, if both feel comfortable doing so.

The effects of the holiday hassles experienced by children of divorce can continue long after they have grown up. I counseled a couple of newlyweds who were on the verge of splitting up after an argument over Christmas arrangements. Julie had told Andrew that she thought it unfair that they had spent only a few hours with her parents and most of the holiday seeing his parents, who were divorced. Andrew had exploded. He was too upset to discuss it or to be supportive of Julie.

During our counseling session, Andrew told me he still felt tremendous pressure to please his parents during the holidays, each of whom still pressured him to spend Christmas with them. He had tried hard to work out a plan that would accommodate his parents and also his new wife and her parents, an overwhelming task. If he had discussed this problem with Julie before the holiday, or asked her to help him work it out, she might have been more sympathetic. But when she complained, he just couldn't handle it emotionally.

Andrew told Julie and me, "Every year I feel like going away by myself for Christmas, so I don't have to deal with them. That's what my sister does."

In addition to ruining Andrew's holidays, his parents' competitiveness almost jeopardized his marriage.

I encourage parents to work out a plan so that the children can enjoy all of their holidays. For the times that parents do not have the children, I suggest they make plans for themselves with friends or family, so that they are not alone. On the following page is a sample holiday chart that can help parents plan holiday arrangements.

If No Agreement Can Be Reached, Seek Help

Parents who find they are quarreling over their children and are unable to settle on a suitable parenting plan should seek help; otherwise their conflict may escalate into a battle that could be traumatic for the children.

Adam, a sensitive ten-year-old boy involved in a hot custody dispute, had witnessed many physical fights between his parents. Bad memories of these fights could remain with him for life.

Holiday and Vacation Schedules

Holiday and vacation schedules take precedence over regular schedules.
Holidays for Mother: Every Mother's Day and Mother's birthday
Holidays for Father: Every Father's Day and Father's birthday

HOLIDAY SCHEDULE	EVEN YEARS	ODD YEARS
New Year's Day	Father	Mother
Presidents' Day Weekend	Mother	Father
Easter	Father	Mother
Passover	Mother	Father
Memorial Day Weekend	Father	Mother
Fourth of July	Mother	Father
Labor Day Weekend	Father	Mother
Halloween	Mother	Father
Thanksgiving	Father	Mother
Chanukah	Mother	Father
Christmas Eve	Father	Mother
Christmas Day	Mother	Father
Child(ren)'s Birthday(s)	Father	Mother
Other		
VACATION SCHEDULE	EVEN YEARS	ODD YEARS
Easter Vacation—1st Half	Father	Mother
Easter Vacation—2nd Half	Mother	Father
Summer Vacation Schedule Two weeks with each parent, to be arranged by agreement, plus additional time for the parent having less time with the children during the school year.		
Christmas Vacation—1st Half	Father	Mother
Christmas Vacation—2nd Half	Mother	Father

On page 110 is the picture Adam drew of the war that was going on between his parents. He drew his mother and father on two battleships, facing and firing at each other. He drew a submarine below the water, between the two battleships, and labeled "the children." He drew a plane overhead, labeled "the counselor" and from the plane he wrote the words, "Stop! Stop!"

In his drawing Adam appeared to be asking me to help him end the war between his parents. This was not an easy task, as his parents had been fighting for years and were deeply entrenched in their own positions. Across the top of his drawing in large letters Adam wrote with black crayon: "THE PROBLEMES WITH DIVORCES IS THEY TURN INTO WOARS."

Susan and John were referred to me for mediation when they were in court litigating visitation issues regarding Adam. John had remarried; Susan had not. They also had a nineteen-year-old daughter who had lived with her boyfriend since the separation and was not involved in the proceedings. Fortunately for Adam, his parents were finally able to reach an amicable agreement after several sessions of child-custody mediation. Difficult as it was for them to meet and to communicate, they persisted until a parenting agreement was reached. They did this out of love for their son. Their struggles and their triumphs are described below.

Adam's parents had been separated two years. During that time, Adam had been living with his mother and seeing his father irregularly, according to his father, and regularly, according to his mother. The parents lived approximately an hour's driving time apart.

At the first meeting, Susan and John sat tensely in my office as I explained the purpose of the mediation session. If they were able to reach an agreement about Adam, a judge would not need to make the decision.

I let them choose who would tell me first his or her perceptions of the situation and give me an idea of what he or she wanted to happen.

John spoke first, grimly. "I have joint custody but the problem is maintaining contact with my son. I am supposed to have reasonable visitation rights, but Susan will only permit me to see Adam three nights a month. She punishes me and uses Adam as a weapon.

This weekend, for example, she refused to let Adam go with me, after I understood I could pick him up. She refuses to help with the driving at all.

"I want more time with Adam, at least what is standard for the courts to allow. I want half of the summer and I want a definite plan so I don't have to beg her for time to see my son."

John proposed the following schedule: alternate weeks from Friday after school until Wednesday at 8:30 A.M., and on other weeks either Monday or Tuesday evening overnight; alternate holidays; one-half of Christmas vacation; one-half of Easter vacation; Father's Day; and his own birthday.

Susan said, "It was very difficult when he left us. I tried hard to do everything for Adam. I took him to a counselor. I even let John use my house, but he abused my privacy. He used my phone and drank my wine."

She continued, "Adam is confused. He is insecure. John took him to San Francisco for his wedding and made Adam fly back on a plane alone. I offered him half of last weekend, but he came at the wrong time. The situation is most serious, the way he uses Adam. He let Adam read the court papers. I can't count on him to pay Adam's medical bills. It is impossible to work anything out with him."

Susan made the following proposal: John could see Adam every other weekend from after school on Friday to Sunday at 7:00 P.M.; one evening a week on the weeks he didn't have Adam for the weekend; one month in the summer; the last week of Christmas vacation; the first half of Easter vacation; Father's Day weekend; and Adam's birthday every other year.

Adam's parents and I discussed the situation and focused on summer plans, since that was their most crucial concern at the time. Together we sketched out a plan and reviewed it with each parent's attorney and Adam's stepmother, all of whom were in the waiting room during the session. It was agreed that Adam would spend six weeks with his father that summer and the remainder of the vacation with his mother. The parent with whom Adam was not living would have him for one twenty-four-hour period each week. Adam's parents agreed to return in two weeks to discuss a permanent parenting plan. I suggested they consider having Adam spend alternate weekends with each of them from Friday after school through Monday morning and one evening every week overnight.

John opened the next session by announcing, "I want a restraining order against Susan dumping on Adam. Susan told him everything that happened in court, and when I picked him up from school the next day, he was mad at me."

Susan blurted out angrily, "He picked Adam up without telling me."

John continued, "Susan gave Adam a distorted idea of what went on. She laid a guilt trip on him. Adam cried because Susan doesn't have the time or money to plan fun things like I do."

Susan retorted, "It's difficult for me without money and Adam sees it. I have court expenses again and John is not paying his bills."

Susan, John, and I discussed the situation. I told them that I could see ways both of them were dumping on Adam.

John said defensively, "I'm forced to counter her constant campaign of alienation against me, so I asked Adam, 'What does your mother pay for?'"

I explained to Susan and John how damaging it was for Adam to hear these negative remarks and to be pressured to take sides with one parent against the other. Adam's parents agreed to a mutual restraining order prohibiting them both from discussing financial issues with Adam and from making derogatory statements, including subtle negative comments, in front of Adam. Afterward Susan said defensively, "I didn't tell Adam everything I could have."

The remainder of the session was used to discuss a parenting plan. John was now willing to have Adam on alternate weekends from Friday through Monday morning, and one evening a week overnight, but Susan still said, "No school nights!"

At this point I suggested they return for another session. From the way they were fighting, I knew Adam must be suffering greatly from their conflict, and I told them I felt it would be helpful and unburdening for Adam to accompany them. They agreed to another session in a few weeks.

On the day of their appointment, Susan and John brought Adam to my office. I briefly explained to the child that the purpose of our meeting was to make things easier for him. I asked him if he would like to draw a picture or read a book while I talked with his parents. Adam took paper and crayons and settled down in the waiting room.

John announced that the summer schedule was working, and Susan said next year she wanted the vacation schedule to be planned ahead so she could enroll Adam for tennis lessons. We discussed this briefly, and I volunteered to help them work on it later. We went together to the waiting room, where Adam showed us a drawing he had made which clearly indicated the pain he was experiencing. His parents and I were deeply touched. There were tears in his parents' eyes.

I escorted Adam into my office, where I asked him what he thought was going on between his parents.

Adam replied, "One wants to do one thing, and the other wants to do another thing. They have big fights. My mom says bad things about my dad, and my dad says bad things about my mom. I don't know who to listen to."

I asked how that made him feel, and he said that it upset him, so that he felt bad all over.

I asked how his living arrangement was working out and he explained that it was okay, but sometimes there was a problem "'cause of mixed-up plans." He described a situation that had occurred recently: "We were visiting my mom's sister. We came home and we were waiting for my dad, but he didn't come. Finally my mother called my dad to see when he was coming, and my dad said he thought that my mom was bringing me to his house. Later on I asked my dad about it, and he told me that my mom was supposed to pick me up, but my mom said my dad was." Adam said this had happened a few times.

I asked, "How do you get along with your mother?" He replied, "Good, she's nice."

Then I asked how Adam got along with his dad, and he said, "I get along good, except when I ask dad questions that my mom asks me to ask him." He explained the questions made his dad a little uptight and that in turn made him feel uncomfortable. He added, "Sometimes I think my dad is wrong, but he tries to convince me that he isn't."

At the end of our interview I asked, "What would you like to see happen now?" and he answered, "I'd like for them to stop saying this and that about each other when I go to each of their houses. I want them to stop getting mad at each other on the phone."

Adam gave me permission to tell his parents what we had talked about, so we invited them in and they listened attentively.

Then Susan and John agreed to return to try to develop a parenting plan that could meet Adam's needs and reduce the acrimony between them for his sake.

On the morning of our next appointment Susan came, but John was late. We waited a few minutes for him, then I escorted Susan into my office, where she told me it was not working out well. John was not cooperating, she said. He had kept Adam on her day off after he had agreed not to. "He does as he pleases," she said. "What can I do? I don't think he will even come today."

At this point I called John, who answered the phone sleepily and explained that he thought the appointment was for later that morning. He apologized, and said he would arrive in thirty minutes.

Meanwhile, Susan told me how touched she was by Adam's drawing. "He has not verbalized this before. I decided never to argue again in front of Adam, but John makes everything so difficult."

I suggested we work out a schedule so things could go more smoothly between them and arguments could be avoided. I suggested that she write John a note when she knew her working schedule, so that he could select days to see Adam when she would be working, not on her days off.

Susan was still apprehensive, "When he doesn't return Adam on my days, what recourse do I have?"

I explained that a good parenting plan would help. She continued to object to Adam spending any school nights with John because he would not cooperate about Adam's homework, and he did not return Adam's clothes.

I suggested that it was Adam's responsibility to do his homework, not hers, and that it was best in most cases for parents to allow their children to take this responsibility themselves. Susan said that in general she agreed, however, Adam had had to repeat kindergarten and be tutored for a year and a half after that. Now it was too costly to continue with the tutoring, and although Adam was very bright, he was slow in doing his homework and needed a parent to supervise him every night. John would not take this responsibility and therefore she wanted Adam home on school nights so she could be sure he did his homework. Also, she told me, Adam was two years behind emotionally.

I told Susan bluntly that if she and John did not stop "warring," Adam would be in much worse shape. I told her I would talk to John about this, and perhaps he would take some responsibility for supervising Adam.

Susan stated that she would be willing to give some responsibility for Adam's education to John, "But he agrees to anything and then he just won't cooperate."

At this point John arrived, and handed me a holiday chart that he had prepared. Both parents were in agreement about all the holidays except Christmas vacation; after some discussion they tentatively agreed to alternate the first and second halves of the vacation.

I then introduced a discussion about regular schedules throughout the year, and began by summarizing Susan's concern about Adam spending school nights with his father. I asked John if he would take responsibility for sitting with Adam on certain school nights and helping him complete homework assignments. John replied that he would. He also brought up the same idea that Susan and I had discussed earlier, namely, that Susan would send John a note listing in advance the days she had to work; then John would select weekdays, when Susan was working, to have Adam. John liked that idea very much.

Both John and Susan asked me to help draft an agreement that they could consider and discuss with their attorneys. They agreed to return in two weeks, at which time they would sign the agreement or make the necessary changes. The three of us drafted the following agreement:

1. The parents would continue to have joint legal custody of Adam.

2. During the school year, Adam would spend the following times with his father: alternate weekends from Friday, 3:00 P.M., to Monday, 8:30 A.M.; one evening each week, when the mother worked, from 3:00 P.M. overnight, through the following morning at 8:30 A.M. Susan agreed to provide John with her schedule in writing two weeks in advance, or less, by mutual agreement.

3. Summer vacation schedule: Adam would spend the first part of summer vacation through August 1 with his mother on even years and with his father on odd years, and the other half with the other parent.

4. Holiday and vacation schedules:
    (a) Holidays for mother: Mother's Day, mother's birthday, and the following holidays on even years: New Year's weekend from December 31 at 6:00 P.M. to noon the day before school begins; Martin Luther King's birthday, July 4, Thanksgiving Day, Lincoln's birthday, Columbus Day, Adam's birthday, the first part of Christmas vacation from the day school lets out through December 26, 8:00 A.M., and the second half of Easter vacation.
    (b) Holidays for father: Father's Day, father's birthday, and the following holidays on even years: Washington's birthday weekend, Memorial Day weekend, Labor Day weekend, Veterans' Day, the second half of Christmas vacation from December 26, 8:00 A.M. through December 31, 6:00 P.M., and the first part of Easter vacation. On odd years, they would switch.

5. The parents were restrained from arguing in front of Adam, making derogatory statements about each other to Adam, and pressuring Adam to take sides on disputed issues.

As they were leaving, each with a copy of the agreement, John said, "I never dreamed we would accomplish so much today. I just didn't expect it." I reminded both of them how happy Adam would be if they could settle their differences, but as they walked down the hall I could hear them arguing over who would pay for Adam's summer classes.

Susan and John spent most of the next session arguing about Adam spending Tuesday nights with John. Susan insisted he would lose too much sleep; John was livid. John said, "I want more time with Adam. I'm not going to give up having Adam at least one night a week. I guess we're going to have to go to court."

I asked Susan to consider that this extra time with John might benefit Adam enough to outweigh his missing a little sleep, but she would not hear of it.

Then I asked them both to consider a compromise: Adam would stay overnight on Tuesday evenings only on the weeks his father did not have him for the weekend. On alternate Tuesdays John would return Adam by 9:00 P.M. John said he would agree to it and so did Susan.

All the issues they had raised had been resolved. Both Susan and John indicated that they were satisfied, and each left with a copy of the revised agreement. No further appointment was set. They would be in touch with me about their final decision after they discussed it with their attorneys.

The morning after our appointment, John telephoned me to say that his attorney would call about the informal wording of the agreement. Otherwise, he was prepared to sign it. John was upset, however, because of an argument he had with Susan the night before about who was to pick up and return Adam. I told him for Adam's sake these arguments had to stop. I suggested they come in again to discuss this and to smooth out some last rough spots. He accepted my suggestion gratefully.

While John was still on the phone, I telephoned Susan on another line. I told her that John was prepared to sign their agreement; Susan said she was too. I also told her that John had mentioned the argument of the night before, and I repeated what I had said to John, "These arguments have to stop." When I mentioned that John was willing to return to my office to discuss this, if she would come, she accepted and warmly thanked me for the help.

Susan telephoned me the day before our appointment to change the date and I called John, who expressed deep frustration: "It's like pulling teeth. All the delays." He agreed to attend our next meeting, but said that if a final agreement was not reached this time he intended to go to court for a solution.

When John and Susan arrived for their appointment, I greeted them warmly and asked each of them what they hoped to accomplish that day. They both said, almost in unison, "To finalize our agreement."

However, John had some issues he wanted to raise. The first was that Susan share half the driving on weekends and vacations.

Susan refused flatly. "That's ridiculous. I don't get home from work on Friday until 6:00 P.M. I'd have to give Adam dinner and I wouldn't be able to get him to your house until 9:00 P.M."

I pointed out to John that he would miss dinner with Adam if Susan brought Adam to him so late. After some thought, John decided to drop the issue.

He then asked to be able to make changes in his schedule should he have to leave town on business and miss his days with Adam. Susan refused to have this in writing, but indicated that she would try to accommodate him. I suggested the following formula, which both accepted: should either parent find it necessary to miss an assigned evening, day, or weekend with Adam because of business commitments, the other parent would make every effort to allow him or her to make up the time missed as soon as possible.

The last issue John had on his agenda was the restraining order against making derogatory statements in Adam's presence. He and his attorney were also requesting that Susan not contact any member of John's family.

Susan responded to this angrily, "I'm friendly with his parents and his sister. I won't be restrained from talking to them. He talks about me too."

They began to argue over this. After a few minutes I said, "I would like to remind you both why you are here—to make life easier for Adam. When either of you makes derogatory statements about the other, it keeps the war going, and that hurts Adam. He wants the war to end."

Susan nodded affirmatively, "It's Adam's birthday today."

I asked, "Wouldn't it be a wonderful birthday present for Adam if you could settle all this today?" Together we wrote the following restraining order: Parents are restrained from arguing with each other in front of Adam, and from making derogatory statements to anyone about the other parent in Adam's presence. Parents shall not discuss disputed issues with Adam or pressure him to take sides.

Now it was Susan's turn to present her agenda. Her first issue dealt with the length of time that each parent could take Adam away on vacation. Susan opted for three weeks, not six as John had requested. She said, "If you want to keep him away longer, I'll probably agree."

John protested. He didn't like the idea of having to ask Susan's permission to keep Adam longer, and he insisted he wanted the six weeks' vacation in writing. After fifteen minutes of argument, I suggested they consider a four-week vacation with an additional two-week option by mutual agreement, consent not to be unreasonably withheld. When they could not agree on this, I suggested splitting the difference and making it twenty-five days. Neither of them liked this, and an impasse developed until Susan said, "Let's skip over this and come back to it later."

Susan then stated that plans must not be made between John and Adam without her knowledge. John had sometimes picked up Adam at school on her day and taken him to buy shoes or sports equipment without telling her. John agreed to telephone her and let her know beforehand. A statement was written incorporating this point.

The only issue still unresolved was Adam's summer vacation. I told them, "You have come a long way. If you can't resolve this issue here, I can write up all that you have agreed to, and you can ask the judge to decide on this one."

John yielded: "I'll settle on a one-month vacation with an option for six weeks, as you suggested."

Susan yielded too: "Okay, I'll go for four weeks."

I spent the next thirty minutes writing up their agreement, while in a calm manner they discussed the anxiety Adam was having entering a new school and making new friends. "I like the way you are discussing Adam together," I told them. "This is the kind of cooperation and support he needs from both of you."

I gave each a copy of the agreement to read carefully and show to their attorneys. I also gave Susan the original; after she signed it, she was to give it to John for signature and he would return it to me. Both of them said I would hear from them in a few days.

A week went by and I discovered that a few minor items, such as the wording of the paragraph pertaining to "missed" days, were holding up their signing.

I suggested an alternate wording and offered to meet again, but they preferred a conference phone call. The items in question were smoothed out in less than half an hour. John and Susan were scheduled to be in court two days later for their financial hearing and they came to my office that morning to sign the agreement.

Hallelujah! I told the two of them, "This is a real triumph for you. It shows how much you both care about Adam." I wished them well and commended their attorneys for their assistance.

How these parents will get along in the future is yet to be seen. This is a great concern of mine, but I firmly believe that the parenting agreement they signed will help keep things running more smoothly for them and for Adam.

As this true story illustrates, a possessive attitude on the part of either parent causes children pain. It can lead to parents' competing with one another; pulling, tugging, and pressuring a child; and even kidnapping the children. A child in the middle of such conflict feels insecure and powerless—trapped in the position of having to choose between parents and tormented by self-hatred and guilt. The longer the parental conflict and competition last, the more pain the child experiences and the greater the chance that his or her self-esteem will suffer. This, in turn, reduces his or her chances for happiness, fulfillment, and success.

Instead of competing, parents can share in raising their children. There is plenty of work and responsibility to go around. There is no scarcity of things to do for growing children and usually no valid reason for one parent to try to have sole responsibility.

Without help, Adam's parents might have gone on competing and fighting indefinitely. If you as a parent find yourself caught in an ongoing battle, or even continual, subtle disagreements over the children, I strongly suggest that you seek divorce mediation or divorce counseling that includes the other parent.

If the other parent refuses to participate, seek help on your own. It will help you learn how to approach and deal with the other parent, and this can make a positive difference for your children. Often, even small changes made by one parent can defuse the situation and bring much needed relief from tension and despair.

6

Rebuilding a Support System for Your Child

A child's universe is shaken when parents separate and divorce. In many cases, in addition to the changes that occur naturally during a separation, important family members disappear from children's lives. It could be a father or a mother, a grandparent, a stepparent, an aunt or uncle or cousin, or a close family friend. One entire side of a child's family may suddenly become unavailable because of parental competition and anger.

The loss of special family members and important relationships is extremely damaging, for children need a family. They need love, support, and reassurance from many special people, particularly at such a difficult time. For their children's sake, parents should make every effort to preserve and foster all of a child's familial relationships, no matter how angry or upset they may be with the other parent and the other parent's family.

Realistically—and ideally—when a marriage or a relationship ends, it is not the end of the family for the children who are involved. The form and structure of the child's family changes: instead of a mother and father together, with family and friends from both sides, the child has two separate parents, along with each parent's family and friends. In time, stepparents—and their families—may become important additions to the child's family. All these people constitute the child's restructured family and are an important support network. It is vital that the child have these people available. The fewer losses a child sustains, the greater the chances for healing and for feelings of security and well-being.

The two configurations on page 122 illustrate the way in which

Child's Family Structure
Before Divorce

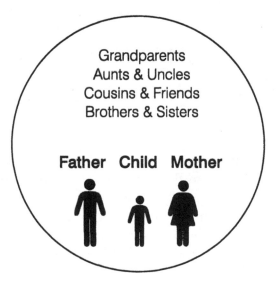

Child's Restructured Family
After Divorce

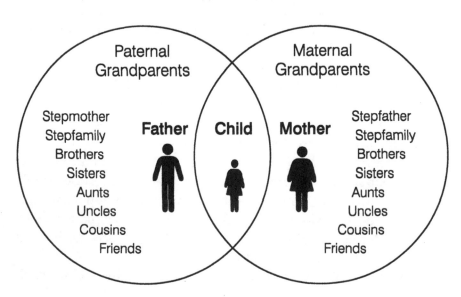

the structure of a child's family changes after divorce, and yet all family members remain available to the child.

Grandparents, relatives, and family friends should be asked by each parent not to make derogatory remarks about the other parent in the child's presence, not to pressure the child to take sides against the other parent, and not to pump the child for information regarding the other parent. They should not question the children as to where they want to live, or discuss legal, financial, or custody issues with them. All family members should be made to understand that these behaviors would harm the children.

Parents who have had a falling-out with their former in-laws and relatives should try to defuse the tension to help avoid family feuds and future problems for the children.

Debbie, a young mother, told me she had never liked her mother-in-law: "She interfered in our marriage. She'd talk to Chris about things but not to me. I don't want her picking up my baby. If Chris can't come and get him, she can't have him."

In a frustrated voice, Chris said, "Debbie, you're not being fair. When I get off work a little late, I need her to pick up the baby. *Your* mother watches the baby while *you* work. I'll go to court if I have to."

I told both parents that if they wanted their child to feel secure, they both needed to be flexible. I pointed out that they had a long time ahead of them during which they needed to work together.

Nevertheless, each of them held strongly to their position. They went to court over this issue, and one can only imagine what grief lies ahead for their child.

A Message to Unwed Parents

The plight of children of unwed parents is especially fragile. Many such children grow up without remembering or ever seeing or knowing their father. Now many unwed fathers want to be involved in their child's life and are reaching out to establish their rights as parents. Whenever possible, unwed fathers should be given access to their child and be included in the child's life. When unwed mothers refuse to acknowledge them as the father, or refuse them access to the child, unwed fathers may find it necessary to go to court to establish their rights legally.

Some unwed fathers experience tremendous pain and frustration in trying to see their children, especially if they cannot afford an attorney, and many give up. James, an unwed father in his early twenties, walked into my office one day and asked for help in seeing his three-year-old son. He said that he and his son's mother, Lynn, had lived together for several years and had separated six months before. With great emotion James said, "Lynn is completely unwilling to let me see my son. Every time I try to see him, she threatens to call the police." He broke down and wept. "This has been so hard for me."

When I suggested he seek legal advice to establish himself as the father and to obtain visitation rights, he explained that he was unemployed and could not afford an attorney. I asked if he had tried to get help through legal aid. He said he had applied but was told they did not take his kind of case; it was they who had referred him to me.

I told James I was willing to call Lynn and ask if she would come to my office to discuss the situation. He enthusiastically accepted my offer. While James waited outside, I phoned her and identified myself as a counselor in the conciliation court. I told her that James was seeking visitation rights to see his child. Lynn became very upset. "James can't see my child. I want nothing to do with him, and if he ever comes around here, I'll call the police."

I asked Lynn if she would be willing to meet with James and me. She was very negative at first, but after we talked a while she agreed.

During the meeting, Lynn was completely against James having any contact with their child. I told her all the things I say to parents regarding the needs of children and the importance of a child having contact with both parents, but everything I said fell on deaf ears, and she walked out.

I suggested to James that he contact a fathers' rights group for assistance in establishing paternity and filing for visitation rights. I gave him the names of several groups.

James learned that he would have to join a group to receive help, but the fee was forty dollars and he did not have the money. I suggested he go to the local law library and research how to file the papers himself. He returned with the information that there were no prepared forms for filing a paternity action; the law librarian said he would have to make up his own. This would involve researching how to write up the "Order to Show Cause" to describe James' situation and his request.

I accompanied James to the county clerk's office, and the file clerk confirmed that anyone wishing to file a paternity action had to seek legal advice or prepare the papers himself. James confessed he could barely read and write, so the situation seemed hopeless: James could not afford legal advice, and he lacked the knowledge, skills, and education to prepare his own legal case. He told me, "I'm going to give up. My son will have to grow up without a father unless Lynn changes her mind." He walked out of the door in tears, and I felt sad that his son may never know him.

Unwed mothers who exclude the father from their child's life may be setting their children up for feelings of rejection, abandonment, and lifelong unhappiness. One adorable three-year-old, Bianca, who had never seen her father, went up to every man she saw and asked, "Are you my daddy?" She might have gone on looking for her daddy her whole life had her mother, Dana, not finally understood that Bianca had a right to know her father. I had explained to Dana that someday Bianca might be very angry when she found out her mother had kept her away from her father.

Dana took this advice to heart and within two weeks called me to arrange a meeting between her and Bianca's father, Gino, to discuss his visiting Bianca. Gino lived in another state, and Dana had not seen him since Bianca's birth. That meeting was extremely difficult for her, as she was still furious with him "for letting Bianca and me down before her birth, after he'd promised to help me." Gino had not wanted to be a father and had changed his mind at the last minute and run away. Dana was left alone at a most difficult time, and she was not yet prepared to forgive Gino. When Bianca was a few months old, Dana took her baby and moved to another state, determined to raise her daughter alone. When Gino tried periodically to see Bianca, Dana refused him access. She was concerned that he would let Bianca down "the way he did me."

During their meeting Dana asked Gino what his intentions were toward their daughter. Was he going to make a commitment to see her regularly? If not, he couldn't see her at all. Gino said he wanted to be Bianca's father. He apologized for his past behavior and offered to give Dana money for Bianca every month. Dana agreed that Gino could see Bianca the following month, but she wanted to prepare Bianca for his visit.

After the first visit, Dana told me, "Gino walked in. Bianca looked at him, walked all the way around him, looked him straight in the eyes very seriously and said, 'You hurt my mommy and me. Why did you do it?' Tears came into Gino's eyes, and he told her how sorry he was for what he had done. He gave her a little gift he had brought. She opened it, and a big smile lit up her face. She took his hand and led him into her room where they played with her toys for an hour and a half."

Gino has visited Bianca every few months since and calls her once a week. On her fifth birthday, both of Bianca's parents took her to Disneyland for the day. Dana describes Bianca's behavior as less restless and irrational since she has been seeing her father. Before that she often woke up in the night screaming inconsolably and thrashing about in anger. Fortunately, Dana was willing to reconsider her former decision, go through this pain from the past, and give her daughter a father.

A Message to Stepparents

If you married a man or woman with a child, you inherited a stepchild and that child's entire family. You are now an important part of this family too, even if it may appear otherwise to you. Your stepchildren may be giving you a difficult time. They may be struggling with feelings of disloyalty to their other parent, and as a result may resist loving you. They could actually be under pressure from the other parent not to accept or enjoy you, or they could be blaming you for the divorce or for taking a parent away from them. The other parent may be feeling threatened by your presence and may be causing you problems. And there are other family members and sensitive issues to deal with. At times, these problems may seem insurmountable.

Your patience and understanding can help your stepchild adjust to you and can ultimately allow you and your spouse to have a closer relationship. The more you can deescalate conflict between your spouse and the other parent, and the better you relate to your stepchild, the more comfortable and happy your own marriage will be.

Bonnie and George's story demonstrates the strain and pressure placed on a marriage when love and support are not forthcoming from a stepparent.

Bonnie and George had been married two years, after living together for six. It was a second marriage for both of them, and they each had one child. After the marriage, Bonnie's ten-year-old son lived with them. George's eighteen-year-old daughter Jill had lived with her mother, and was now living with her husband of one year.

Bonnie was thinking of separating from George because of their problems over Jill, which began even before they were married. Bonnie came in alone to see me, and began angrily. "Three years ago, George forced me to have Jill live with us. We had a small apartment, and we were already very crowded. I said no, but he brought her in anyway." She explained that this had occurred just after Jill had dropped out of high school. George was concerned about her and had planned to enroll her in a special school near their home. "His plan didn't work because Jill wouldn't get up for school. It was an awful situation, and I asked both of them to leave. George and I were separated for a while, then we got back together."

Then, after Jill's engagement, Bonnie and George argued over financing her wedding. "I was shocked when I found out how much it would cost. We didn't have that kind of money. George told me he wouldn't pay more than twenty-five hundred dollars, but I knew it would go way over that. And that's the way it is even now—I just can't trust him to keep his word. He goes behind my back to do things for Jill. The last straw was his giving Jill the bed he bought for her when she moved in with us. I told him no, but he gave it to her anyway. He ignores my feelings. I can't depend on him to make me his first priority." Bonnie said that when she confronted George about the bed, he told her that he couldn't stand the stress, so he had given it to Jill. "It's easier for him to say no to me than to Jill," Bonnie said.

Power struggles and stresses of this kind are deadly to a marriage. Even if a stepparent "wins," he or she loses. A stepparent should avoid placing the natural parent in the position of having to choose between the stepparent and his or her own children. In most cases, the children "win," because the bond that exists between a parent and child is so strong. Trying to come between a parent and child is like trying to hold back a mighty river.

When I explained this to Bonnie, she, having a child of her own, understood. She had expected George to put her needs before his daughter's, and when he didn't, she was furious. Stepparents are wise to join forces with the natural parent in caring for the children. The more compassion and support stepparents give to their stepchildren, the more love they are likely to get from their new spouse.

Many stepparents play primary roles in raising their stepchildren, especially when their spouse has primary custody or joint custody. These stepparents should encourage their stepchildren to maintain a positive relationship with the other parent, as it would be in everyone's best interest. The stepchildren will feel better about themselves and have fewer problems, and the stepparents will be happier and freer to enjoy their new marriage.

Jeff, now fifteen, was raised by his father and stepmother since he was three. He is now fifteen. Jeff's parents divorced when he was a year old. He lived with his mother, Carolyn, until he was three. Then Carolyn felt unable to care for him, because she was going through a difficult time emotionally and she thought Jeff would be better off with his father, Andrew, and his new stepmother, Monica. Carolyn told me that almost immediately Monica took over the role of Jeff's mother and squeezed Carolyn out of Jeff's life. For example, Monica had Jeff call her "mommy." After being refused access to Jeff time after time, Carolyn ran away, because the pain and frustration became too much for her. Periodically, she called and was hung up on, or dropped by to see Jeff when she came to town but was refused access. It took her years to save the money to take

Andrew to court for visitation rights. By this time Jeff was so angry at her for abandoning him that he did not want to see her.

Meanwhile, Jeff was having serious learning and behavioral problems, and was eventually placed in a school for emotionally disturbed children. I met with the entire family and encouraged Monica and Andrew to help their son establish a relationship with Carolyn. They reluctantly agreed, provided Jeff wanted a relationship with his mother.

When I spoke to Jeff, he regarded me sullenly. "I'm afraid to give Carolyn a chance. She might run out on me again, and then I might mess up again at school. She didn't want me. She just wanted to do her own thing. That was more important to her. I'd like to get to know her, but I'm not sure how I'd feel. Maybe I'd screw up again. I don't want to get upset. I'd love to see her, but I'm worried. How will I react? I'm doing better at school now. I want it to stay the same. I'd like things to stay the same and be able to see her."

I told Jeff he was older now, and stronger; he could stand up for himself. I encouraged him to begin seeing Carolyn for short visits, to talk to her on the telephone every week, and see how that went. The next week he called Carolyn and they arranged to meet for lunch; Jeff then agreed to meet her once a week for dinner. He told her he was worried about how Monica would take it, but that he did want to see her.

Children need the freedom to enjoy and love all members of their family. Jeff need not have suffered the way he did had his stepmother been wiser and more understanding.

As a stepparent, you can help keep peace by not competing with the other parent, and by reassuring your opposite that you respect him or her as the child's parent and that you only want to be helpful and are not trying to usurp his or her position.

Stepparents can benefit from reading books on stepparenting. Stepparenting groups are available in some areas, and help can be found at counseling agencies and divorce-mediation centers.

A Message to Grandparents

Grandparents: you are extremely important to your grandchild. No one who can give a child an ego boost quite as well as a doting grandparent. It might be of interest to note that in California a law makes it possible for grandparents to seek visitation rights in court.

Your grandchildren need your love, support, and protection. I say protection because some grandparents take sides and add to the tension caused by divorce by speaking ill of their former daughter- or son-in-law in front of their grandchild. One little girl told me sadly, "I don't want to see my grandma anymore. She always says bad things about my mommy. It makes me feel bad. I wish she would stop."

Divorce is heartbreaking for grandparents, but in spite of your own disappointment and sadness, your help is needed to make peace for your grandchild's sake. You can help your grandchild by promoting peace between his or her parents and encouraging your grandchild to remain neutral. In addition, you can be a calming influence and offer as much help to both parents as you can. You will be doing this for your grandchild out of love, and also bringing peace of mind to yourself.

7

Creating a Closer Relationship with Your Child

To help your child do well in life, the best gift you can give him or her is a close, loving relationship. The twelve guidelines below can help you achieve this closeness and make your child feel loved.

1. *Become a good listener.* Even if you don't agree with what your child is saying, be willing to listen without interrupting and then discuss the problem afterward. This will enable your child to feel he or she can talk to you.

2. *Allow your child to express feelings,* even hostile, angry feelings, and allow him or her to cry. This will help your child feel comfortable around you.

3. *Comfort and reassure your child* when he or she is upset. This will establish feelings of security and of being loved by you.

4. *Be demonstrative—show your affection for your child.* Be free with your hugs and kisses and, whenever appropriate, tell your child that you love him or her. This will establish a loving closeness between you.

5. *Protect your child from parental disputes or disagreements.* If you involve the child, it will make him or her feel insecure and uncomfortable around you.

6. *Set reasonable rules and limits for your child's behavior according to his or her age and development.* In time this will help him or her to see you as fair and reasonable. It is not unusual

for young children to have temper tantrums when they don't get their way. Allow them to cry, kick, or scream without being punished or given their way. Gradually your child will learn your rules and what behavior you expect.

7. *Along with discipline, give your child as much praise as you can.* Your child will grow up feeling good about herself or himself. Avoid corporal punishment of any kind: slapping, grabbing, hitting, beating, shaking, choking, or any other action that might make your child fear you. Harsh punishment can weaken your child's ego and destroy your chances for a close relationship. Avoid threatening to punish your child or to send her or him away. Also avoid prolonged punishments, such as long periods of being grounded or deprived of privileges.

8. *Do not call your child names or use put-downs.* These can cause a child to feel unloved, uneasy, and insecure. It may also make him or her overly sensitive and spoil his or her capacity to develop friendships.

9. *Set realistic goals for your child,* and try not to have unrealistic expectations based on what *you* wanted out of life. Do not make your child feel guilty about disappointing you, for this could make him or her feel like a bad person and uncomfortable or sad in your presence.

10. *Avoid excessive behavior around your child* especially drug use and alcohol abuse. If you have a drinking or drug abuse problem, be honest with yourself about it and get help. Children become very frightened when parents are out of control. Your child will dread being around you and eventually will not want to see you at all.

11. *Take time to play with your child.* Choose activities geared to your child's age and interests. Children enjoy a wide variety of activities: picnics, walks, biking, games, cooking. There are also inexpensive places to take children, such as parks, beaches, the zoo, or museums, and occasionally including

one of your child's friends can increase the enjoyment. For young children, avoid activities that involve long periods of sitting.

12. *Gradually, patiently, and with love, help your child to learn and grow in knowledge, skills, and independence.* The better your child feels about himself or herself, the better he or she will feel about you.

Parenting After the Divorce

The guidelines above are basic for developing closer parent-child relationships. The additional thoughts below can minimize the risk of your child feeling abandoned, caught in the middle, or helpless, and of you losing trust, love, and affection.

See your child as soon as possible after the separation

If parents decide to separate, arrangements should be made for the children to see and spend time with each parent as soon as possible. Many children are very anxious when a parent moves out of the home. They should be taken as soon as possible to visit the parent's new home and be given a telephone number so they can contact that parent whenever they feel the need to do so.

Some young children feel very guilty when their parents separate, believing that in some unexplained way they caused the divorce. They need reassurance that the divorce is not because of them, and that the parent who leaves will not disappear from their lives. They need to hear words like, "Mommy [or daddy] and I are not going to live together anymore, but I will still see you a lot [or whenever I can, or on Sundays or weekends]. I will be calling you to say hello and find out how you are doing. I love you and I will always be your mommy [or daddy]." A few simple words like these will let your child know he or she is not losing you.

Despite such reassurance, some children will continue to feel insecure. They will test their parents to make sure they are still loved and won't be cast aside, for often they fear their parents may divorce them, too. They may misbehave to put parents to the test. Although parents may become exasperated at such behavior, they should avoid threatening to send the children away, or saying things in anger such as, "I don't want you here anymore!" It is far more helpful for parents to very clearly tell the children to stop what they are doing, while letting them know at the next opportunity that they still love them. A combination of firmness and affection lets children know their parents will not abandon them, but that their parents *will* set reasonable limits for their behavior.

Encourage your child to have a positive relationship with the other parent

A relationship with a stepparent cannot make up for the loss of a parent. Since young children do not understand adult problems, when they become estranged from a parent they experience this as not being loved, or as being forgotten, ignored, neglected, rejected, or abandoned. They tend to blame themselves and feel unlovable. They think to themselves, "If I were worth loving, then my daddy [or mommy] would love me and want to be with me. Since my daddy [or mommy] doesn't see me or spend time with me, it must be because I am not worth loving." These negative feelings diminish a child's chances for success and happiness.

For this reason, if for no other, in addition to nurturing your own relationship with your child, encourage your child to have a positive relationship with the other parent. You will be promoting that relationship for the sake of your child, not for the other parent.

Mary and Ali's story demonstrates the great unhappiness that can be caused by trying to punish a former spouse.

Chris and Mark were only one and three years old when their parents separated. It was their mother, Mary, who left their father, Ali, "to get away from Ali's domineering and controlling ways." Mary said that she left the boys with Ali because she couldn't possibly support them. A few months later she found a job and wanted to take the children, but Ali wouldn't talk to her or allow her to see the boys. She found an attorney and took Ali to court, where he was awarded custody and Mary was given visitation rights on alternate weekends and alternate holidays.

Ali reluctantly complied with the court order, but he kept the battle going. He was extremely bitter toward Mary for leaving him and the children, and he let his sons know it.

Four years later, in an attempt to obtain custody of her sons, Mary took Ali to court again. I met with them in the conciliation court, but when the situation was not resolved, a custody investigation was ordered. The investigator recommended that the children remain with Ali and that Mary have liberal visitation rights.

Mary tried to get custody of the children again six years later. This time I met with both the parents and the children. Mark was now thirteen, and Chris was eleven. Before interviewing the children, I conferred with the parents. With great emotion Mary told me, "Ali is constantly trying to turn the boys against me. His bitterness has increased since my remarriage. I want full custody so he won't turn them against me. He can see them on alternate weekends."

Ali replied angrily, "I've had the boys since they were babies. She left them, and now she wants them back. The investigator recommended that they remain with me. When she left she talked about putting them in a foster home, so I took them. I can't stand a mother who would give her kids away."

I talked to Ali and Mary about how hard conflicts of this kind are on children, especially when they continue over a period of years. My concern appeared to fall on deaf ears. Then I asked to speak to each of the boys alone. Chris volunteered to go first.

I asked Chris, "What do you think is going on between your parents?"

Chris answered, "It's bad. My mom wants to be friends, but my dad doesn't—because my mom left us."

I asked Chris how his parents' conflict made him feel. "I feel uncomfortable and nervous."

I then asked Chris, "How do you feel about your mother leaving you when you were little?"

"Pretty bad."

"Why do you think she left you?"

He answered, "Probably when we were little we couldn't do work for her. Now we could."

When I asked Chris, "Do you think your mother loves you?" he answered, "She loves me a little bit." He added, "The man across the street told me my mom was filthy. He's very honest."

I asked Chris, "What would you like to see happen now?"

Chris replied, "I want my mom and dad to get along and no more fighting."

I thanked him for talking to me and got his permission to share what we talked about with his parents.

Mark was next, and he told me, "My dad doesn't want to talk to my mom, but she wants to talk to him. Our neighbor agrees with my dad, because she didn't want us. I was three."

I asked Mark if he remembered living with his mother.

"I can't remember, but my dad told us she didn't want us. My mom said she didn't have any money to have us. My dad says, 'Go ask the neighbor.' My mom says he's lying. I don't know what to believe."

I asked, "How does all this make you feel?"

"I feel sad about the divorce and I feel bad my mom left us."

When I asked Mark if he believed his mother loved him, he answered, "Now I think she cares about us, but not before." He said he had a bad feeling about her leaving, "but she probably had a good reason. I don't believe anyone would just do something like that. Now she wants us back. My dad says she's unfit. I don't think she'll get us."

Mark showed me a notarized letter he wrote for the court. "My dad wanted me to write it. I don't like to write what my mom or dad do wrong. It makes me feel bad." The letter he had written stated: "I want to live with my father. He has always taken care of me. My mother never wanted us. She wanted us put in a foster home."

After the children's interviews, I talked with Ali alone. We discussed his anger and bitterness and the way it was affecting his sons. Ali agreed to stop bad-mouthing Mary in front of his sons.

I asked Ali what his own childhood had been like. He said he had left home at thirteen after his mother abandoned him to an alcoholic stepfather who beat him. Ali had not forgiven his own mother for leaving him, and he was not willing to allow his sons to feel loved by their mother either.

Children who suffer from feelings of abandonment tend to have low self-esteem, which they carry with them into adulthood. Ali has transmitted the pain he experienced as a child to his sons. If no change occurs for the better, his sons will in turn pass it on to their children. This is a tragic example of the damage done to many children of divorce. Because of Chris' assumption that his mother did not want or love him, he will feel less worthwhile, less loved, and be less likely to succeed in life.

Ali could have spared his children years of pain. He could have tried to normalize the situation a month after the separation, before this tremendous psychological harm was done to his sons. But Ali was thinking of his own disappointment and the pain of losing Mary, not of what his sons needed. If he had been thinking of his sons, he would have encouraged Mary to spend time with them. He would have been willing to communicate with her about the children and to cooperate in working out a schedule to allow both of them to be involved in raising their children.

Instead, he made the boys feel all the more abandoned, rejected, and unloved by constantly reminding them that their mother had left them and did not want them. He even involved a neighbor to back him up. In short, Ali allowed his bitterness against Mary to lessen his sons' chances for a good life.

Ali paid a price himself for holding on to his bitterness all those years. Holding grudges saps a person's energy and vitality and in the end brings little satisfaction. The questions one should ask oneself are: Is it worth holding onto my anger? Is it worth sacrificing my own life and the lives of my children?

It is essential that parents get off to a good start when they decide to separate, or at least soon thereafter. Parents should make every effort to correct a bad situation, or they will be storing up terrible misery for themselves and their children.

See your child regularly

It is through frequent, ongoing contact that your child will feel loved and cared for. The younger the child, the more frequent your visits should be. Some parents put off seeing their children because they are "too busy" making a living or building a new life, or too preoccupied with their own survival. Their children are not their main priority at this time. These parents may believe they will be able to spend more time with their children later, without realizing that when later comes, their children may not want to see them. The children may have been feeling hurt and rejected, and to protect themselves from this pain, they may reject that parent in return.

If you live far away and cannot see your child often, there are ways of keeping in touch. See your child as often as you can. Even sporadic visits are better than no visits at all. One of the worst feelings a child can deal with is that of having been forgotten, rejected, and abandoned by a parent. Phone calls, thoughtful cards, notes, and small gifts will help your child feel loved.

Gain your child's trust

To your child, security means being able to count on both parents. To build their trust, keep promises you make to your children.

Billy, five years old, waited in the driveway of his mother's residence one Friday afternoon. He had his bag packed for the weekend and was anxiously looking out for his father, who had promised to pick him up at five o'clock. At six, his mother called for Billy because it was getting dark. Billy refused to go into the house. "Daddy will come. He told me he would." At six-thirty, he came into the house sobbing with disappointment. His father hadn't come and hadn't called. His mother had to hold Billy for an hour to calm him down.

Disappointments such as these undermine a child's security. Once a child loses trust in a parent, it is difficult to rebuild it. Therefore, parents should not make promises to their children they cannot keep.

When you must change or cancel your plans, call beforehand and notify the other parent. It is best also to speak to your child. A simple explanation can be very reassuring, such as: "I can't come tomorrow to pick you up. I am sick [or I have to work, or I'll be out of town]. I am sorry, because I'll miss you. I'll be coming to pick you up on Sunday. I love you. I'll see you soon." These small acts of consideration help spare children hours and days of feeling rejected.

Don't try to turn your child against the other parent

Barbara and Alan, divorcing parents of two teenage daughters, were ordered to talk to me when they were in court fighting over their children. Their attorneys warned me that Barbara was making it difficult for Alan to see the girls or even talk to them because of her anger regarding Alan's girlfriend.

I escorted the two parents into my office, leaving their daughters in the waiting room. Barbara began by telling me that Alan's girlfriend, Julia, had been in a fight with the older daughter, Pamela, age sixteen, and had slapped her. Barbara insisted that Alan see his daughters alone and not with Julia. She told me, "Julia has no right to touch my child." With an angry look at Alan, she added, "The girls are very upset about Alan's unfaithfulness."

Alan began, "I grew up without a father, because he was always busy working. I spent a lot of time with my children. We were very close. I miss this close relationship now. I've been very depressed. I feel abandoned by them. Barbara has threatened to turn them away from me." Tears came to his eyes. "I feel sad and guilty about leaving them and about not being close." He said that he had left Barbara twice before because of all the arguments. "Our marriage was never right. We got married because Barbara was pregnant." Alan said he wasn't willing to exclude Julia when his daughters were with him. When I asked him about the fight between Julia and Pamela, Alan said, "Pamela was mean to Julia because of all the bad things Barbara tells her about Julia and me."

They exchanged angry words for a few minutes. I spoke to them about the importance of not transmitting any more of their anger and pain to their daughters.

Next I saw Pamela. She told me that her parents argued constantly over money, bills, and custody. When I asked her how that made her feel, she replied, "It makes me feel like, why can't they settle everything and not just keep fighting. It upsets me because my mother takes her anger out on me. She screams at me, and there is a lot of fighting going on in the house because of her anger." Pamela said that at times she felt very confused and had severe headaches. She said she saw her father whenever he was available and she could make it, but that her mother questioned her incessantly about her father and his girlfriend. "It makes me feel very uncomfortable. I can't see my father without being questioned. I dread going back to her house and being questioned. She doesn't want me to see my dad."

I asked Pamela how she got along with her father and Julia. "I get along fine with my dad and fine with Julia off and on. We have some arguments, usually about my dad spending money on me; otherwise it's fine." I asked her if it was all right for Julia to be there when she was with her father and she said yes. Pamela's idea about what caused the fight was that "Julia tries to run his life and tell him what to do—about buying me things, but later we talked about it and now it is fine, off and on."

I asked Pamela what she wanted to see happen. "Just to get the divorce over and get everything settled. I want both my parents to be happy. I want to live with my mom as long as everything goes well, and I'd like to see my dad twice or three times a week."

Next I interviewed Pamela's fifteen-year-old sister, Andrea. Andrea told me, "There's a lot of unnecessary hostility and acting foolish. They just fight and argue about little things and about money. It upsets me and makes me think how stupid it is for them to do that. It makes me feel pressured."

I asked her where she felt that pressure in her body. "I feel it in my head and in my heart. It's frustration and pressure—kind of a pain. I feel love for both of my parents."

Andrea said that she and her mother got along fairly well. "We have some arguments about me cleaning up—the basics. We haven't had any arguments recently about me seeing my dad, just her comments. I don't blame her in a way. Dad has money and we don't." Andrea said she and her father got along well, but that she had never liked Julia. "My mom wouldn't want us to like her. It's my choice though."

I asked her if she thought that liking Julia would be a betrayal of her mother. "It would be like betraying my mom right now, but not later on. I understand why my mom feels hurt. I try to make her feel better. I hug and kiss her in the morning to make her feel better."

Regarding her father, Andrea said, "I want to see him once on the weekend and once during the week and on special occasions. I hope it will be okay with my mom for me to see my dad. I'd see him anyway. He's still my father." She said there were certain things she could talk to her father about, just as there were other things she preferred discussing with her mother. She ended our talk by saying, "I want the divorce thing to be fair and for them to be friends."

I brought the whole family together for a conference. At one point Barbara blurted out to her daughters, "You know I hate your father and wish he were dead."

I told Barbara, "You're feeling a lot of hurt, anger, and hatred toward Alan right now. Do you love your girls?"

Barbara replied, "I love them more than my own life."

"I know you love them," I responded, "but do you love them enough to want to spare them any more pain? This has been very hard on them. They have been experiencing a lot of strain and pain and they need relief. Are you willing to stop questioning them and stop making negative comments about their father and Julia in front of them? Are you willing to do this for them?"

Barbara looked down. Then she nodded her head affirmatively and said yes. As they left, I hoped that Barbara would be firm in her resolution for the sake of her daughters.

Do not pressure your child to choose where he or she wants to live

One of the most painful and confusing dilemmas to a child is to be asked to choose between mother and father. This causes a child to feel extremely insecure, especially when the issue of where he or she is going to live remains unresolved.

Tracy's parents had been quarreling over custody of Tracy since she was two years old. They came to see me when Tracy was twelve. When I asked Tracy how her parents' constant fighting over her made her feel, she replied sadly, "I wish I were never born. Then they wouldn't have to fight."

Randy, a ten-year-old, who had lived with his mother since his parents separated three years before, said he felt extremely uncomfortable when his father asked him to live with him. "I was afraid to tell him I wanted to stay with my mom. I was afraid he'd be mad at me. I didn't know what to tell him, so I didn't say anything. I didn't want to hurt him."

These children are obviously under great pressure. Children should not have to endure this kind of pain.

Avoid discussion with your child of legal and financial matters pertaining to the divorce

When I interview children, some of them tell me of statements their parents have made. One six-year-old girl told me angrily, "My daddy is making it hard for my mommy. He wants to sell the house. Then we won't have any place to live." A fourteen-year-old boy said, "I feel like an attorney. My mom tells me one thing; my dad tells me something else. I don't know what to believe."

Children have enough problems dealing with the emotional aspects of divorce and all the changes in their lives brought about by divorce. They don't need the extra burden of being told all the legal and financial details.

Cooperate when there is an emergency or crisis

Accidents and emergencies are bound to arise. When they do, children need the cooperation of both parents more than ever. Animosity and blaming between parents just makes things harder.

Ron, the father of five-year-old Justin, made an appointment to see me alone. I had seen Ron and his wife together previously. Ron told me there had been an accident. Justin had fallen off the top bunk-bed in the middle of the night and fractured his wrist. Ron admitted that Justin's bunk bed had no safety bar. After the accident, instead of calling Justin's mother, Judy, Ron had called his girlfriend to drive them to the emergency room. Two hours later, after their return, he called Judy.

"Judy was furious with me for not calling her sooner. She yelled at me on the phone, and said, 'I'm his mother. You caused this accident, you idiot.' She went on and on, swearing at me."

Ron hung up on her, but Judy called back a minute later. Ron tried to tell her that he needed to schedule a morning appointment with an orthopedist, but he couldn't get a word in. Ron hung up again. She called him back, and this time they managed to make arrangements to meet at the doctor's office in the morning.

Ron held Justin while his girlfriend drove. Ron said he asked Justin if he would like his father with him at the doctor's office, and when Justin said yes, Ron told him, "Your mom yells at me a lot, and I don't like it. I never yell at her. If she yells at me in the doctor's office, I'll leave."

When they all met at the doctor's office, Ron said he "tried to introduce my girlfriend to Judy, but Judy called her a whore and called me a bastard over and over again in front of Justin. I asked her to stop. I pointed to Justin, but Judy said, 'I want him to know what a bastard you are.' She's trying to make me look bad in front of my son. What does she tell Justin about me when I'm not there? Sometimes I feel like throwing my arms up and going away. But I can't. I want time with my son. I think it's the court's fault for giving custody only to one parent instead of joint custody."

I felt great empathy for Ron, but I told him I understood why Judy was so upset. She should have been notified sooner so she could have come at once to the emergency room.

Ron replied, "When Justin fell down and cut his head open and had to have stitches, she never called me at all."

I replied, "And how did that make you feel? You are his father. Two wrongs don't make a right."

I suggested that perhaps a joint session with Judy to discuss the incident and to make plans for handling future emergencies might be useful. I encouraged Ron to learn from his mistakes and to be open rather than defensive if we got together.

Ron clearly had some responsibility for the accident and for Judy's anger, but during an emergency it is urgent that parents work together. Justin's injury was enough for him to deal with at the time without the added pain of witnessing a fight between his parents.

Seek help for your child if red-flag symptoms persist

Many conditions are "red flags" that children may need professional help, especially if they persist. As indicated earlier, sleep disturbances, asthma, allergies, bedwetting, tantrums, tics or other repetitive behaviors, teeth grinding, vomiting, clinging behavior, overaggression, daydreaming, withdrawal from relationships, overeating or loss of appetite, diminished school performance, delinquent behavior, self-destructive behavior, drug abuse, frequent crying, absence of emotion, difficulty talking about feelings, and siding with one parent against the other are all cause for concern.

These behaviors may spring from depression or anxiety resulting from the divorce and parental conflict as well as the losses and changes in the child's life. Most children respond quickly to help, especially when parents cooperate about a treatment plan. Serious consequences can result if these symptoms are ignored or if parents refuse to cooperate.

Jennifer, five years old, was an allergic and asthmatic child. Her mother, Vivian, gave her prescribed allergy medicine on a regular basis, which seemed to lessen the frequency and severity of the asthmatic attacks. Her father, Mark, did not believe Jennifer had a problem. He did not want Vivian telling him what to do. He refused to consult with Jennifer's doctor or to give Jennifer any medicine when she was with him. To make matters worse, Mark had cats, to which Jennifer was highly allergic.

One night Mark rushed Jennifer to the hospital. She was gasping for air, and they barely made it in time to save her. After this near-tragedy, Mark and Vivian consulted with Jennifer's doctor together. Mark was instructed on how to help Jennifer and how to prevent recurrence of a severe attack.

It is unfortunate that it might take almost losing a child for some parents to realize that their child's health is more important that winning an argument with the other parent.

When it comes to children's well-being and potential for success, nothing can be more important than feeling secure, loved, and cared about by both of their parents. It is my hope that the guidelines discussed here will help you create the close and loving relationship you and your child need.

8

Child-Custody Mediation

Each year, over one million mothers and fathers divorce. Approximately one million children are involved. In most of these cases, custody and visitation issues are not litigated. The decisions made by these parents are not always in the best interests of their children, however. Some parents have an extremely difficult time accepting the fact that they will have to deal with the other parent after the divorce. Their squabbles can continue year after year.

Before and during the separation period, many parents expose their children to massive doses of anger and conflict. This causes children great pain. Even after the separation or divorce, many children continue to be plagued by parental conflict. Some children are asked to choose between their parents; some are snatched back and forth; some are used as pawns to hurt or punish the other parent; and some lose contact with one of their parents entirely.

Children caught up in a divorce often feel that their whole world is falling apart. Many are alone in their anguish: they look to their parents for support and reassurance, but find their parents too upset to focus on their needs at all.

In approximately 85 percent of divorce cases, issues of child custody and visitation are not contested in court. When parents do litigate these issues, their disputes have traditionally been tried by the adversary system; such terms as *custody* and *visitation* come to family law directly from criminal law. According to the adversary system, each parent must prove that he or she is the better parent— usually by making the other parent look bad, wrong, or unfit. Custody litigation proceedings aggravate family situations: they create more acrimony between parents, more pain for the children, and an escalating hostility that may never end.

Since 1981, California has required mediation prior to trial for all parents who are litigating child-custody or visitation matters. This much-needed intervention minimizes the hurt to children and families by giving parents a chance to settle their differences with the help of a neutral third party. Not only has child-custody mediation proved to be cost-effective by saving valuable court time, but it has been highly successful in helping families resolve conflicts. Even when agreements are not reached, the knowledge gained during mediation can help families later on. Requiring mediation gives parents self-determination: they can choose between settling their conflicts on their own or letting the court decide. Many parents opt for settling.

Mediation is a viable alternative to litigation and a valuable tool for resolving family conflicts. This chapter is about the mediation process in action, presented out of my experience as a counselor and mediator. It portrays a complete description of what mediation is and what you can expect to gain from mediation.

The Mediation Choice

Separation and divorce are stress-filled times. Parents can easily allow themselves to lose control and be run by their emotions. They need to exercise great restraint to curtail hostile actions and remarks in their children's presence. It takes great courage for parents to recognize attitudes and behaviors that are detrimental to children, such as thinking of children as "mine" rather than "ours," keeping children away from the other parent to punish him or her, using children to gain a better financial settlement, controlling the time children spend with the other parent, competing over children, not seeing children regularly, arguing in front of the children, asking children to choose sides, and continuing to bring up the past.

Some parents believe the court can settle their problems regarding children. Instead, litigation often leads to more litigation, especially when parents are dissatisfied with what has been ordered in court. Some parents return year after year, trying to resolve their conflicts, not realizing that the courtroom is not the place to solve these disputes.

Some parents think they can win in court. Unless children end up with two involved parents, everyone loses. Children need two parents who are willing to work together to raise them, and to share time and responsibility for their care.

When parents cooperate after separation and divorce, children have a far better chance of healing, of feeling more self-confident, of having higher self-esteem, and of feeling more reassured about the future.

Besides benefiting children, mediation offers parents several important advantages. These include reduced frustration and hostility, less re-litigation, more satisfaction with the process, and substantial savings of both time and money.

Mediation is increasingly popular as a means of resolving divorce and separation issues. It is quicker and cheaper than a court trial, and it helps reduce the hostility and bitterness generated by the adversary system. The adversary process focuses on the past and encourages competition; mediation focuses on the future and encourages cooperation. The voluntary choice of both parties to work together is what mediation relies upon. Since both parties actively participate, the settlement reached is often better suited to meet the family's needs than an order handed down by a judge.

Custody and visitation mediation is already available in many areas of the United States and is continually reaching more people. Custody mediation is practiced in courts, mediation centers, and family therapy clinics. It is used by therapists and mediators in private practice, by attorneys, by attorney-therapist teams, and in churches.

Ordinarily, the role of the attorney is to represent only the rights and the best interests of his or her client. However, in family law matters, the two adversaries are usually *parents-in-common:* their children's well-being depends on a settlement of their dispute. Attorneys can serve their clients best by toning down their adversary posture and supporting their clients in settling their differences in as amicable a way as possible.

When and How to Use Mediation

Mediation is a powerful and effective process. It can help parents settle their differences at any stage of the divorce proceedings. However, the sooner parents avail themselves of it, the less possibility of the conflict escalating, and the less likelihood of trauma for the children. Many risks can be avoided when guidelines are established early on and parents feel reassured they are not going to lose contact with their children.

Attorneys can put things into perspective for clients who are too distraught to do so themselves. They can encourage clients to separate financial issues from custody issues; they can help parents to understand that children are not property and do not go with the house. They can explain some of the benefits of cooperating about children, such as a greater likelihood that both parents will remain involved, a better outcome for the children, and less chance of conflicts and litigation after the divorce.

When divorcing parents behave destructively or irresponsibly toward the children or former spouses, or make unreasonable demands in court, attorneys can ask them to reflect on the high price of keeping the battle going. Both parents and their children endure continuous pain and suffering as long as the dispute is unresolved. Many family counseling services offer pre- and post-divorce counseling. Attorneys can encourage their clients to seek help for themselves and their family, so the choices they make can be curative rather than destructive.

An appointment for an exploratory session with a mediator can be arranged by attorneys or by the parents directly. When attorneys represent parents, parents can be instructed to discuss whatever agreements are reached during the mediation session with their attorneys before finalizing the agreements. Some mediators include attorneys in certain portions of the mediation process, such as at the beginning or toward the end. Agreements reached by parents with a mediator can be written up as stipulations by attorneys or by the parents themselves and submitted to the court for filing, therefore making it into a legal court order.

What to Expect from Mediation

The primary purpose of mediation is to reduce hostility between the parents and thus to secure and enhance the health, welfare, and well-being of the children. As a mediator, I accomplish this by assisting, supporting, and encouraging parents to work together to provide a safe and nurturing environment for their children. Focusing on their children's needs, they can develop a workable parenting plan. Their children can then experience close and continuous contact with both parents after separation and divorce.

The goals of mediation

To establish a more cooperative, less combative relationship for parents—and ease and enhance life for their children—I have set the following general goals for my counseling sessions:

1. To provide a safe, nonadversarial setting in which parents can discuss and resolve issues and differences.

2. To give everyone present the opportunity to speak and be heard.

3. To help parents disentangle spousal roles from parental roles so they can focus on their children's needs.

4. To help parents focus on the present instead of the past.

5. To give parents the opportunity to discuss issues, to explore alternatives, and to find ways of resolving differences.

6. To give parents and children the opportunity to hear some information and input from me.

7. To encourage parents to settle issues amicably and cooperate about their children.

8. To encourage self-determination.

9. To encourage frequent and ongoing contact between children and both parents.

10. To encourage open and direct communication between parents about the children.

11. To encourage a supportive, cooperative family network for the children that includes parents, stepparents, grandparents, and extended family.

12. To help parents work out a parenting plan, consistent with their children's needs.

13. To enable parents to make changes over time.

14. To refer families for counseling as needed.

The role of the mediator

Mediators have many different styles and approaches. Some handle only custody and visitation issues; others deal with financial issues as well. Some work alone; others work in teams. Some work in private practice; others, in agencies and courts. Some see only parents; others, entire families. Some see families for only a few hours, others work with families through many sessions. Differences in style, approach, and philosophy are not important here. The outcome for the children and family is. A skillful counselor, therapist, or mediator can effect a positive change in parental attitudes that will benefit children.

In my own approach, I serve families in three capacities: as a counselor, as an educator, and as a mediator.

As a counselor, I facilitate expression of feelings, concerns, and wishes. This promotes freer, more effective communication between spouses and between parents and children. I help parents to become aware of their attitudes, beliefs, behavior, and communication patterns that interfere with satisfying family relationships and personal growth. I encourage them to acknowledge their own responsibility for the way things have been in the past, and help them focus on the present and future. I try to reduce family conflict and tension and to prevent further psychosocial damage to the children and family.

As an educator, I focus on teaching parents about the process of divorce and about their children's needs. For many people, the mere notion of having to relate to their former spouse after the divorce comes as a complete shock. I carefully explain that divorce ends marriage, not parental relationships.

In mediation, I discuss the concept of divorce as a process, not as a single event. I explain that parents and children need time to go through its many phases. Although custody and visitation disputes are very difficult and painful for children, children can heal from divorce when parents cooperate.

Children are dependent upon parents to create a safe and harmonious environment for them, and they need reassurance from both parents that they are still loved and will be taken care of. Children also need close and continuous contact with both parents, and they need permission to love both parents and other important people in their lives, such as stepparents and grandparents.

In my role as educator, I explain that there can be negative consequences when children lose a relationship with one parent after separation or divorce. Children often experience this loss as rejection or abandonment, and feelings of rejection or abandonment can lead to lowered self-esteem. Children need to feel at home in each parent's house, and they need both parents to remain involved in their lives.

Even if the marital relationship was extremely difficult, parents can learn to cooperate and develop a working relationship where the children are concerned. Part of this cooperation is avoiding behavior that is painful and damaging for children: fighting, arguing, or violent scenes in front of them, making derogatory statements about the other parent, pumping children for information, sending angry messages through children, putting children in the middle, asking children to choose between parents, competing over children, keeping children away from the other parent, snatching children back and forth.

I explain that any plan parents choose should meet the children's needs and suit the family as a whole. The plan must ensure that the children's education is not interrupted. Agreements should be kept by both parents so that they come to trust each other, and parenting plans should be re-evaluated periodically and necessary changes made to meet children's and parents' changing needs.

When talking with parents, I stress cooperation rather than competition. I explain that having some flexibility is important. Parents should try to accommodate each other whenever possible to make *occasional* changes or special arrangements.

I also educate children about divorce. I tell them that divorce is not the end of their family, and that they are not losing either of their parents. Their parents are not leaving or divorcing them; they are leaving or divorcing each other.

I assure children that although everyone is very upset now, things will calm down. I explain that the process may take time, but that what happens is up to their parents—the divorce is not their fault, and it is not their job to get their parents back together.

I also reassure children that their parents will not stop loving them, and that they will be cared for. I explain that in most cases, children have the chance to see both parents. And I tell them that it is all right to continue loving both parents and not take sides, and that it is all right to love everyone: stepparents, grandparents, and other family members—on both sides of the family.

As a mediator, I serve the parents as a neutral third party who works for neither parent. I help each parent, keeping the welfare and needs of their children in mind. I facilitate communication, clarification, and discussion of issues that need to be resolved. We then explore possible agreements. I encourage parents to focus on the present and future instead of on the past. Finally, I help them develop a parenting plan consistent with their children's needs.

How long does mediation last?

The length of each session varies, depending on the amount of time I have available, the amount of time the family has available, the progress being made, and the willingness of the parents to continue. I see most families for one session lasting from two to three and a half hours.

The number of sessions also varies, depending on the progress toward resolution and on the willingness and availability of the parents to continue. The parents are aware that about one-third of families return for a second session. I have seen only a small number of families for a third or fourth session and only a few families for more than four. I refer people to resources in the community should they desire ongoing professional help.

Interviewing family members

In addition to parents, children and other family members are often included in the sessions. After meeting briefly with the entire family, I ask the children to sit in the waiting room while I interview their parents. This spares the children from experiencing unnecessary conflict, pressure, or pain. After the parental conference, I interview each child separately.

When stepparents, grandparents, or persons living in a parent's home are present, I include them toward the end of the session, focusing on the children and their perceptions of the parental conflict. Including these important family members promotes more willingness on all their parts to join in an amicable solution to the conflict.

The First Mediation Session

When parents first arrive for mediation, they are usually nervous, apprehensive, and tense—they believe their situation is hopeless. This hopelessness stems from the frustration of dealing with the other parent during the years of marriage and since the separation and divorce. Often, feelings are still raw. Each knows how to push the other's buttons.

To serve the whole family, the mediator must remain a neutral third party to whom everyone can relate. As a mediator, I am faced with the dilemma of having to be both supportive and confrontational with one or both parents when necessary. I present myself as a caring person, and make known to everyone my desire to assist them in resolving their conflict. I explain that most parents feel hopeless when they first come in but many reach an agreement. I believe I will be able to help them, and I think they sense this.

When children are present, I show them where their parents will be so they won't worry. Then I give them crayons and paper and show them to the room where they will wait until the parental interviews end. To begin the session, I ask parents six basic questions to clarify the reasons for mediation:

1. Has the divorce been finalized?

2. Is this issue we're going to discuss about custody or visitation?

3. How long ago did you and your spouse separate physically?

4. Where have the children been living since the separation?

5. How often have the children been seeing the other parent?

6. Who initiated this court action—or, in pre-divorce situations, who filed for divorce?

Sometimes parents argue over answers to these questions. I defuse tension here by explaining that we will be discussing all this at length in a few minutes.

I explain to the parents that the courtroom is not always the best place to settle family problems, and I explain the mediation option:

"This is an opportunity for you to discuss the children and to see if I can help you reach an agreement between yourselves, instead of the court making these decisions for you. You will always be the parents of these children. It's far better for them and for you if you can learn to work together. You don't have to like each other or live together. You only have to learn to work together as parents. This service is confidential. I'm not an investigator, and I don't make recommendations to the court. If you should reach an agreement, I can write it up for you, your attorneys can check it over and guide you, and the agreement can become your own court order. Changes can be made in your agreement later, as long as you both agree on them. If you don't reach an agreement here, you can return to court and let the court decide for you."

Some parents believe that if the judge orders something, everything will be settled. I explain that no one really wins in court. If one parent isn't satisfied with the court order, he or she can keep returning to court, but the children usually sense the parent's dissatisfaction with what the judge has ordered.

Sometimes I tell parents about a young man I interviewed when he and his parents were referred to me. He was almost eighteen years old. He told me with tears in his eyes that his parents divorced when he was six and have been fighting over him ever since. "I wish I could set the clock back," he said. "My whole childhood has been ruined." I tell parents that this young man may never be happy. He has come to expect life to be terrible. I want to help parents realize the negative consequences of keeping their battle going and to explode their belief that things will all be settled in court.

For the first hour or so I interview the parents. I prefer to see them together because it also enhances communication between them and helps eliminate each parent's suspicions about what was said behind closed doors. Only on request of the parents do I interview them separately. Parents usually prefer to remain in the room while the other spouse is being interviewed, even though it is sometimes difficult not to interrupt. Not interrupting is a ground rule.

Occasionally one parent gets very upset about something the other parent has said and interrupts. In a friendly manner, I give that parent the choice of leaving the room until the other parent has finished or remaining quiet. In my years as a mediator, only a handful of parents have chosen to leave. Most of these left for only a few minutes and then returned on their own and sat quietly.

Parents decide who will go first, and each parent speaks for about twenty minutes. I focus on the parent who is speaking and loosely guide the interview. I ask, "How do you see the situation?" Some parents go through the history of the marriage, outlining what they believe went wrong. Some blame themselves; some blame the other. Some express a lot of emotion; some express a desire for a reconciliation. Some have trouble focusing on the children at all; some begin talking about the children immediately.

Each parent is given the opportunity of being heard completely. Some say it is the first time they have had a chance to express themselves, because the other parent would never let them talk or would never listen. Some parents tell, with tears in their eyes, of their deep frustration and difficulty in trying to communicate with the other parent. Whatever else happens in the session, at least this much is accomplished.

I also ask each parent, "What would you like to see happen now? If you could write your own court order, what would it say?" By the time the interviews are over, I have an idea of how each parent sees the situation and what each parent's "ideal" parenting plan is. No matter how far apart parents are in their views or positions, or how hopeless their situation may seem, I remain optimistic. A positive attitude can make the difference between being able to help parents reach an agreement and not being able to.

The parental interviews are followed by a brief free-for-all discussion period: a time for parents to talk together with no input from me. Parents usually spend this time arguing over what one has said or defending themselves against statements the other has made.

After five or ten minutes, I call a halt to the arguing and summarize the issues each parent has raised regarding the children. Whatever situations or issues the parents have presented, I work with them toward a resolution. I put into perspective what each parent wants for their children. I discuss children's needs, the distance between parents' homes, parents' work schedules, special circumstances, childcare, school, and the children's activities. I suggest possible alternatives. Each alternative is discussed, discarded, or accepted—in part or in whole—until one alternative is agreed upon.

I also introduce additional issues, such as vacation schedules, holiday schedules, telephone contact with the children, notification of the other parent in case of serious problems, provisions for making changes or additional arrangements, and other items that could become problems later on if they are not discussed and settled beforehand. I try to smooth out as many rough spots as possible to make the arrangements easy for parents and children.

Throughout the negotiations, I have the children and their needs in mind. In that sense, I am not unbiased. As parents discuss each issue, I gently guide the discussion and speak up on the children's behalf when something is suggested that is not compatible with the needs of their children—for example, a parent settling for not seeing a child or a plan that would interfere with a child's education. In such cases, I suggest alternatives that would better suit their children's needs.

Together, we resolve issues one at a time, by mutual give-and-take and compromise. We often either reach an agreement or agree to return for another session and continue to work on it. Some parents decide they prefer to return to court, but with their attorneys' encouragement and suggestions, many parents are later able to reach an agreement. When parents do reach an agreement or are considering a certain plan, I write up a rough draft.

When parents reach an agreement

Once parents have reached an agreement or a partial agreement, I summarize what they have agreed upon, where they still disagree, what they are considering, and what alternatives have been suggested.

At this point in the mediation, attorneys—if they are present—are included. Only information about the parenting agreement is shared with attorneys; everything else that was discussed during the parental conference is kept confidential. When parents still disagree on significant issues, I ask the attorneys for suggestions. Sometimes they ask for a brief break in the conference to explore unresolved issues with their clients. They often return with either an acceptance of the other parent's proposal or an alternate proposal.

When an agreement is reached, I review the rough draft with parents and attorneys, then write it up for them. Agreements range in length from a few sentences to several pages. I keep the language of the agreement as simple as possible, so less chance exists for misunderstandings and arguments about how it should be interpreted. I begin with a simple custody statement of which parent will have custody, or that they will have joint custody. Then I record the parenting plan, which states when children will be with each parent. This is usually followed by a vacation schedule and a holiday schedule. Then I add whatever behavioral guidelines or specific items parents have agreed to include.

When parents reach only a temporary agreement, I write "Temporary agreement pending further order of the court, without prejudice to either party," across the top. This type of agreement allows parents to try out a parenting plan without too much concern that what they have agreed to will affect their position in court. I often include a return appointment date, at which time I see how their plan is working out and whether a pending court hearing can be avoided.

Each parent reviews the agreement, signs it, and receives a copy. In court-connected mediation agencies, a judge's or commissioner's signature is added to the agreement to make it an official, binding court order. Parents who reach an agreement with the assistance of a private mediator can ask an attorney to draw up the stipulations and present it to the court.

The sample parenting plan below includes a custody statement, a parenting arrangement, a vacation and holiday schedule, and a behavioral clause.

We, Maria Tyler and Noah Tyler, parents of Jonathan, born on June 10, 1984, and of Lisa, born on February 7, 1989, agree on the following parenting plan:

1. Joint-legal custody and joint-physical custody of John and Lisa.

2. Parenting Plan During the School Year
   The children will live with mother and spend alternate weekends with father from Friday after school through Monday at 8:30 A.M., beginning May 7, 1994; and every Wednesday from 5:30 P.M. to Thursday, 8:30 A.M.

3. Parenting Plan During Summer Vacation
   The children will live with father and spend alternate weekends with mother from Friday, 6 P.M., through Monday, 7:30 A.M.; and every Wednesday from 6 P.M. to Thursday, 7:30 A.M.

4. Vacation Schedule
   a. Each parent may have a vacation period with the children for two weeks during the summer, upon 30 days prior notification to the other parent.

b. Each parent will have the children for alternating halves of winter vacation each year beginning with the first half for mother in 1994 and on even years; and alternating halves of spring vacation each year beginning with the first half for father in 1995 and on odd years.

5. Holiday Schedule

a. The children will spend every Mother's Day and mother's birthday with mother and every Father's Day and father's birthday with father.

b. Holidays for mother

On even years: Children's birthdays, Memorial Day weekend, Fourth of July, Thanksgiving Day, and Christmas Eve.

And on odd years: Washington's birthday weekend, Easter Sunday, Labor Day weekend, and Christmas Day.

c. Holidays for father

On odd years: Children's birthdays, Memorial Day weekend, Fourth of July, Thanksgiving Day, and Christmas Eve.

And on even years: Washington's birthday weekend, Easter Sunday, Labor Day weekend, and Christmas Day.

6. Parents agree not to argue in front of the children or make derogatory statements about the other parent in the presence of the children.

_____

Date

_____

Signature

_____

Signature

_____

Witness

Sometimes, one parent wants to sign the agreement and the other wants to think it over. I give them all the time they need to decide: they can take the agreement with them and send it back signed or unsigned; come in and sign it at another time; or schedule another session. If a parent seems dissatisfied, or expresses feelings of helplessness, of being trapped, or of being badgered into accepting an agreement, I explain that she or he has choices and should discuss them with her or his attorney. We often discuss that parent's feelings and possible changes in the agreement that would result in one that is more acceptable. Some agreements make one simple statement, such as, "Parents agree to participate in family counseling at [a particular agency] and return on [a particular date] to discuss a parenting plan." This gives spouses time to work on their parenting with each other, and on relationships with their children, with professional help. Later on, they may come to a suitable agreement.

In some cases, it is important to interview the children before we work out an agreement. Children's input can not only give parents perspective on their own situation, but help them focus on their children's needs. Even when parents are far from an agreement, I encourage them to return with their children or to seek family counseling. This gives children some support and perspective into their situation and their parents' conflict—especially where they are exposed to a lot of hostility—and sometimes softens parents' adversarial stance and helps them to settle their differences.

Once an agreement has been reached, I commend parents and encourage them to keep their agreement so they can build trust as parents, and I remind them that they can renegotiate when their needs and situations change.

The Second Mediation Session

I suggest a second session when parents require more time to discuss, develop, or complete a parenting plan. If the stepparents were not at the first session, I encourage them to come for the second. If the children were not at the first session, I ask parents to bring them.

The children are often having their own problems. They may be upset or confused by the divorce and want to be heard. They may be unwilling to see one parent or having a difficult relationship with one or both parents. They may be showing emotional or physical symptoms. Sometimes I sense that the children are under great pressure from parents, and I want them to have a chance to talk to me about it. At times when I am making no headway with parents, input from the children can help parents to settle their disagreements.

When possible, several hours are set aside for the family. This allows time first to briefly see the entire family, then to meet with parents (and stepparents), to interview each child separately, to meet with the entire family again, to meet with parents and stepparents again, and finally, to develop and write up a parenting plan, should one be reached.

I begin the second session by bringing everyone into my office for a brief meeting, enabling the children to become familiar with my office before their separate interviews.

I take a moment and explain to the children that the reason they are here is to see if I can help their parents work together so things can be easier for them. I explain that I will talk to their parents for a few minutes while they are in the waiting room, and that they can use the crayons and paper I furnish to draw a picture if they like. When I finish talking to their parents, I will ask to talk to each of them for a few minutes.

I work with parents first to find out what has happened since our first session. Sometimes they have changed their attitudes or behavior; sometimes circumstances have changed. This is also a time for stepparents to be heard, especially if they were not present during the first session. Parents decide between themselves who will go first. When one parent has finished, I ask the other to begin. After the second parent has finished, I encourage stepparents to add anything they wish. I allow a brief time for parents and stepparents to discuss issues, then explain that we can continue the discussion after the family conference later in the session. At that time parents might be more focused on their children's needs, especially after hearing what their children have to say. I then escort parents to the waiting room.

The children's interviews

I conduct interviews with children to find out what they think, how they feel, what they remember, how they experience what's going on now, and what they wish to see happen. Even though each child experiences divorce in a unique way, there are feelings shared by many children (see *References*, 4). Many divorcing parents have the same emotions: disbelief, anger, fear, anxiety, guilt, sadness, depression, powerlessness, and helplessness. Children and parents who finally accept the divorce as a reality are better able to get on with their lives. Ultimately my purpose is to lessen tension for children and to assist parents in working cooperatively for the children.

I interview children four years and older, but even younger children are included in family conferences. Children interviews may place additional distress on children initially, but I have found that children benefit greatly from the method I use and appear to go away less burdened.

I let the children decide between themselves who will go first. I interview each child individually, since each experiences the divorce and relationships with parents differently, and this gives each child the opportunity to express how she or he feels without being influenced by what siblings say.

If the child has made a drawing, I admire it and tape it to the wall: children feel good when they see their drawing hung. I ask the child to take a seat and I sit opposite him or her.

I usually start out by asking children what they think is going on between their parents? Most children answer that their parents don't get along or that they argue or fight a lot. Some children say their parents are fighting about who they will live with, or about money, or children support, or mommy's boyfriend. Each child's response gives me insight into how much he or she has been told and exposed to and his or her understanding of parental conflicts.

Next I ask how all this makes the child feel. She or he usually answers "bad" or "sad" or "scared." Occasionally, a child will say that he or she doesn't care.

I ask children why they think their parents are getting a divorce. Some say they don't know why. Others blame one parent for the divorce, repeating something the other parent said. One young child replied seriously, "It's because my mommy kept kicking my daddy out of bed." Another child believed it was because her parents disagreed.

Another question I ask is how the child's parents got along when they were living together. Some children say that they were too young and do not remember when their parents lived together. Some say they don't remember anything but fighting and arguing. A few describe witnessing physical violence between their parents; police coming; or hiding, crying, or trying helplessly to separate their parents physically.

Next I ask (even if I already know) where they live now and how often they see the other parent. Some volunteer that they like the arrangement the way it is. Some do not like it and wish it could be different. If they don't offer an opinion, I ask how the arrangement is working. Many children say they wish they could see their other parent more. Adolescents often talk about their preferences at length; some complain angrily about having plans with friends disrupted. One adolescent boy said, "I want to be able to go when I want to go and not be made to go if I don't want to go."

I ask children how they get along with each parent. They usually describe their relationships simply as "fine," "good," "OK," or "OK, I guess." When I note hesitation or a telling look on their face, I ask if there are things that upset them. Some children describe the problems they are having with one or both parents. Here, again, adolescents tend to speak more about their problems. Occasionally a child will complain about one parent, mimicking the words and tone of voice of the other parent.

I then ask children what they think is going to happen now. Some say they don't know; others express a desire to live with one parent or the other.

Next I ask what the child wishes would happen now. Some children say they want mom and dad to get back together again. When I ask if they think this will happen, most say that they do not think so. Almost all children say they wish their parents would stop fighting and get along better.

Finally, I ask whether children will give me permission to tell their parents what we talked about when we have our family meeting. Most children give their permission. If children feel uncomfortable about sharing their emotions with their parents, I ask what part they wouldn't want their parents to hear and I remember not to disclose it during the family conference.

I then ask what the child thinks would happen if the parents knew how the child felt. The child usually thinks one parent might get mad or feel bad. Some children are afraid they might get yelled at; or, occasionally, punished. I encourage them to let their parents know how they feel. Most children reconsider, but I respect the child's decision either way. In the few cases where the child does not give me permission, I encourage the family to seek family counseling to improve communication between parents and children.

The family conference

Once the last child has been interviewed, I invite the family back into my office. The family sits in a circle, and every child and adult has a chair. The family conference is a very special time for children; some children are nervous about having both parents in the same room. Once everyone is seated, I tell parents that the family conference is a time for the children to share what is going on with them and a time for parents to listen.

To prepare parents for accepting their children's feelings, and to help children feel more comfortable with their emotions, I talk briefly about feelings. Directing my comments to the parents, I say:

Your children have given me permission to tell you what we talked about. Before I share their feelings, I want to explain a little about feelings. People can't help feeling what they feel. Feelings just come to a person. If I'm feeling hungry, I'm hungry. You can tell me, "Don't be hungry," or "You shouldn't be hungry, you just ate," or "It isn't time to be hungry—it's only ten o'clock," but I still feel hungry. The same is true with anger. If I'm angry, I'm angry. Sometimes it helps to tell someone how you feel. Feelings can also change from moment to moment: people can feel angry one moment and not angry the next, especially when they have a chance to tell other people the way they feel.

I then summarize each child's conference in the order the children were interviewed. I reflect back feelings to the child and ask him or her to let me know if I don't say things just right. I then thank the child for sharing with me and with his or her parents.

After the children's interviews have been summarized, I direct my comments to the entire family. I let the children know they do not have to take sides, that it is all right to love both their parents and everybody in their life who is good to them, and that it won't be up to them to decide what happens: it is up to their parents to work it out, or, if their parents cannot work it out, the court will decide what will happen.

I explain that children feel very uncomfortable about having to choose between their parents by saying, "If they choose Mom, they feel they will hurt Dad, and if they choose Dad, they feel they will hurt Mom. They lose either way."

When a child has expressed a lot of anger toward one parent, or when I sense that the child is being pressured by one parent or is siding with one parent excessively, I do some repair work. I encourage the child to meet with the "rejected" parent and me without the other parent being present. This gives the child and the parent a better chance of resolving difficulties without interference. I also suggest such a special parent-child session when I sense the rejected parent might have a harder time hearing negative feedback from his or her child with the other parent in the room.

Some children, totally unwilling to see a parent prior to such a parent-child session, will agree to begin seeing that parent again. Some of these encounters are very touching.

One ten-year-old girl told her father angrily, "If you loved me, you would have tried to get custody of me." Her father cried and told his daughter how much he has missed her and wanted her to be with him. They wept and hugged each other. The mother was then included. Considering the negative consequences when a parent and child drift apart, this was time well spent.

Once the family conference is over, the children return to the waiting room so their parents and I can discuss the situation and try to work things out. If the children have not drawn a picture yet, I offer them paper and crayons and encourage them to make a drawing for my office. I often observe the differences in the children's faces, voices, and body language after the family conference compared with when they first entered my office. They often appear less burdened and anxious, although they are still concerned about whether things will be settled.

Once most parents realize how much their children are being hurt by their negative attitudes and behavior, they are more willing to negotiate and work out an agreement, even if this means compromising. It is not uncommon for even the most hard-nosed parent to soften after the family conference and be willing to reach an agreement.

When the children are told that their parents have reached an agreement, they often get very excited. If the atmosphere is relatively calm between parents, I invite the children in while I write up their parents' agreement. Some children literally jump for joy in their relief and excitement.

The Third and Subsequent Mediation Sessions

Only occasionally do I see a family for a third session. I suggest a third session in cases where all key family members were not available for the other two sessions or when parents still need more time to discuss and resolve certain important issues pertaining to their parenting plan. Sometimes parents who have been to family counseling return to work out a parenting plan.

I ask each parent what has been happening since the last session and what thoughts each has had about what was discussed at that meeting. I encourage parents and stepparents to discuss their unresolved issues freely, and offer little guidance. Usually by the third session, communications skills between parents have improved: they are able to talk face-to-face about their feelings and about issues. I then guide the negotiations until each issue is resolved.

In cases where a key family member, such as a parent, stepparent, or grandparent, was not available before this session, I interview that person and summarize the key issues for him or her. If children are present and have not been interviewed before, I interview them.

After the interviews, I hold a family conference. If an agreement is reached during the third session, I write it up.

I schedule further sessions when one or both parents telephone me complaining about problems they are having or when changes in circumstances require that changes be made in the parenting plan. I encourage parents to discuss what is happening and to look for resolutions to their difficulties. Sometimes such a conference results in a modification of their original agreement or a mutual resolve to continue with their original agreement. When parents are having continual problems, I suggest they consider family counseling.

━━━━━━

As families go through divorce and post-divorce litigation, the stress on family members—especially children—can be overwhelming. The courtroom is hardly the place to resolve deep-seated emotional issues. Child-custody mediation provides helpful intervention at a time when parents are least likely to be focusing on their children's needs. The last thing children need is two parents fighting over them. Unless children end up with two involved parents after the divorce, everyone loses—especially the children.

When parents cooperate, children are more likely to find happiness and satisfaction. For many parents, the transition between being married and being parents-in-common is very difficult. Professional assistance at that time can often protect children from being exposed to years of continual hostility and conflict.

Custody and visitation mediation helps many families to resolve their disputes over the children and to develop an appropriate parenting plan. Even when parents do not reach an agreement, some are later able to put the information they gain in mediation to use. Children are also fortified by the perspective about the divorce and parental conflict that they have gained. This can help them remain neutral and feel less anxious, frightened, and tense.

9

Handling Difficult Situations

Every family's experience of divorce is unique, but certain delicate and difficult situations recur among divorcing and divorced parents and their children. This chapter explores how I, as a mediator, handle these situations. The ideas and suggestions here are only a first step toward improving a difficult situation; I would urge you to consider professional help to address your particular concerns.

Custody and Visitation Issues

One or both parents want sole custody

It is not uncommon for a parent facing divorce to feel threatened about losing contact with his or her children or about losing control over raising the children, and so seek sole custody. Other parents genuinely believe that it is in the children's best interests for one parent to have custody while the other has visitation rights. Still other parents seek sole custody thinking it can give them certain financial advantages. Sole custody is not always the best answer, however.

When one parent files for sole custody, the other parent often feels threatened and responds by filing for sole custody as well. The custody disputes that follow generate hostility between the parents and create a lot of tension for the children, who are put in the middle. Custody battles can last for many years, and to make matters worse, parents often feel more hostile toward each other when they are settled than when they began. This makes it more difficult for them to work together regarding the children, and causes more suffering for the children.

When one or both parents seek sole custody, joint custody is the usual solution. Some parents are initially against joint custody: they think it will not be good for their children to be bounced from parent to parent, or that it will be impossible to work with the other parent, or that the other parent will use it to control or harass the first parent. Many parents have misconceptions about what joint custody means: they think the child would have to live with each parent for six months each year.

Joint custody is not only natural but beneficial both for children and for their parents. According to Isolina Ricci, author of *Mom's House, Dad's House,* children need "two homes with no fighting" after separation and divorce, one with their mother and one with their father. Children tend to do best when both parents remain actively involved in their children's lives. Both are parents before the divorce, and the idea that one parent gets custody and the other rarely sees the children is unnatural and unfair (see *References,* 5).

When parents live near each other, possible options for joint custody include having children alternate between parents daily, every few days, half of the week, weekly, or biweekly; spending weekdays with one parent and weekends with the other; spending alternate weekends and two days each week with each parent; spending more time during the school year with one parent and more time with the other during the summer and school vacations; spending days with one and nights with the other, a good option for families in which one parent works days and the other works nights. In some joint-custody arrangements, the children remain in the family home and the parents rotate caring for the children there. Whatever agreement is made, I encourage as much contact as possible with each parent.

When parents live far apart, possible options for joint custody are spending the school year with one parent and summers and other school vacations with the other, with additional access whenever the other parent can arrange to visit; alternating every school year; or alternating every two or three years. However, I suggest that younger children see their parents at more frequent intervals.

One parent says the children need one home

Some parents want to limit the amount of time their children stay with the other parent because they believe that shuttling back and forth is too disruptive and confusing for their children. They want their children to have one home so their children can feel secure.

When a parent expresses this concern, I explain that having two homes is natural after separation or divorce. A child's security does not lie in being tucked into the same little bed every night. Some people live in one home all their life and still end up very insecure. A child's security usually lies in having a close relationship with both parents: children need to feel loved and taken care of by each of them. I suggest that parents provide a place in each of their homes for their children's clothing, belongings, toys, and books; a study corner; and a toothbrush. Children should be encouraged to develop friends in both places. I urge parents to consider a parenting plan that maximizes both parents' time and input with their children.

A child has lost contact with a parent

When a child has lost contact with one parent for a long time, or does not remember one parent—as with babies or very young children—it is important that he or she is not traumatized by the reintroduction to the parent. I arrange a gradual plan that begins with the children spending a few hours with the estranged parent in the presence of a neutral person with whom the child is familiar. This meeting is held in a neutral setting, such as a park, or another mutually agreeable place. Time with the child is expanded in gradual increments, progressing from an hour, to a few hours, to an entire day, an overnight, entire weekends, vacation periods, alternate holidays, and so on.

The relationship between the child and the estranged parent should be reestablished as soon as possible. The longer parents wait to do this, the more traumatic it can be for the child. The primary parent may at first find it difficult to let the child go, especially if the child is an infant, as parents can be extremely protective and attached to very young children. After the first few meetings, it should become easier.

In one extreme situation I worked with, a ten-year-old had not seen her father since she was six months old. Weekly visitations had been ordered by the court two months prior to my meeting the family. In my work with them, I first interviewed the parents together. The father told me why he had not tried to see his daughter after he and his wife had separated. At that time, his wife had stolen money from him and was trying to prove him insane. He said he could not see his daughter because he was afraid of what his wife might do next. The mother said that at the time of separation, her husband was making threats against her and the baby, so she had ordered a psychiatric evaluation. The father had not shown up for the evaluation. She said that now her daughter cries bitterly when she has to go with her father.

Next, I saw the daughter alone. The child told me of her great distress and great hatred for her father:

> I don't even know him, and I don't want to know him. Why did he have to come back now? Why doesn't he just leave me and my mom alone? I've gone with him twice already and I don't want to see him. He's a terrible man. He just wants to make me unhappy. I hate him—I hate him! I wish he'd just go away and leave me alone.

Surprisingly, the daughter then added, "I only want to go with him three times a month, not every week, so I can have one Sunday at home with my mother."

During a special parent-child conference without the mother present (and with the child's permission), I summarized the child's interview for her father. I then facilitated communication between them. The father willingly agreed to see his daughter three times a month. She had the opportunity of being listened to by her father and of experiencing him as someone who was willing to work with her.

When the mother was included in this family conference, I discussed what the child and father had agreed upon. The daughter then told her mother she would not make such a big fuss about going with her father anymore.

A child refuses to see a parent

When a child refuses to see a parent, or whenever there appears to be a seriously troubled parent-child relationship, I urge the parents to participate in family counseling. There are psychologists, social workers, family counselors, and family-service agencies in most communities who can assist with this situation.

I wish to stress the importance of correcting or improving a poor parent-child relationship. Unsatisfying parent-child relationships often have serious consequences. Poor parent-child relationships can lower a child's self-esteem, and children often repeat the negative patterns of parent-child interaction later on in their lives.

A parent is not seeing a child

When a parent has not been seeing a child and is reluctant to make such a commitment, I explore the reasons why.

Sometimes a parent believes it is too painful for the child to see him or her and then have to separate again. One divorcing father of a four-year-old girl told me he was seeing his daughter on alternate weekends. When it was time to drop her off, she would cry and hang on to him pathetically. This upset the father so much that he thought it might be best if he didn't see her at all. I explained that his daughter was probably having a difficult time seeing him so infrequently, and when she did see him, it was hard for her to give him up. I suggested that he arrange to see her more often—perhaps for two hours one evening a week, or overnight—and call her at least once a week to say hello. If he were to stop seeing his daughter, I explained, she would be absolutely heartbroken and would probably never get over that hurt.

There are many other reasons parents will not see a child. Some have difficulty accepting the divorce and find it too painful to see the former spouse. As difficult as this may be, I strongly urge them not to abandon their child, because the child will never get over it. Some parents have so many hassles with the other parent every time visitation is attempted that they give up trying. For these parents, I suggest divorce counseling, which is available at public and private counseling agencies. For other parents, it is just too painful to see the child and then have to separate again. And sometimes, parents feel very fearful about their own ability to survive the divorce and feel that they must think only of themselves now. For these parents, I strongly suggest they get individual counseling. This can facilitate working though their pain and help them to be more available for their children, who need them desperately at this time although they may not always say so.

Some parents say they cannot see the children because they lack the time, the money, or the transportation; because of their difficult work schedule; or because they live too far away. Regardless of the reasons given, I emphasize that parents look for ways of working it so the children can see the other parent—even if it means that parents share the cost of the transportation, drive halfway, or be more flexible about schedules and arrangements. It may even be necessary, in cases of illness or dire financial hardship, for one parent to provide all the transportation so that the children can see the other parent. Children's needs should come first.

I often suggest individual counseling for parents who feel they just cannot handle seeing the children, and I strongly urge them to make a commitment to seeing the children again. When a child feels abandoned by a parent, that child may never get over the feeling of rejection.

One parent wants to punish the other

Sometimes parents refuse the other access to the children, or make it difficult for the other to see the children, to punish the other parent for the divorce, for hurting them, or for not being a more involved parent. Parents have given many reasons for not wanting their children to see the other parent: "He left us"; "She was the one who wanted the divorce"; "He never pays child support"; "She talks against me to the children"; "I raised the children all by myself and now that they are older I want to enjoy them"; "He wants to enjoy them after I did all the work"; "She doesn't deserve to see them."

Some parents want to limit visitation rights because they claim the other parent "was never involved with the child." Even if a parent was uninvolved with the children before, I urge parents to focus on the children's present needs. Children need frequent contact with both parents—*especially* if this has not been the case. I encourage the parent who has not been involved with the children to take a more active role so that the children can develop a close relationship with both parents. Children do not understand adult problems. They usually feel rejected and abandoned when a parent does not see them for *whatever* reason. Even worse, they often believe they are worthless or not worth loving; otherwise, they reason, their parent would want to see them.

Sometimes, parents want to limit the amount of time the children spend with the other parent because of differences in their parenting styles: the other parent "has a different lifestyle"; "has different values"; "is too strict"; "is too unaffectionate"; "is too lenient"; "is too critical"; "is too insensitive"; "has different rules"; "feeds the children junk food"; "doesn't put the children to bed at a decent hour"; "doesn't give the children a bath"; "doesn't make them brush their teeth"; "doesn't make them do their homework." The concerned parent may be worried that the children will be harmed or confused by these differences. In my discussions with these parents, I explain that what confuses or harms children most is when parents do not respect each other's right to be different. This puts children in the middle and creates a lot of tension and problems for them. Differences in parents and parenting are natural. Even when parents remain together, they don't always agree on how to raise children. Children learn to handle these diversities and to discover what they can expect from each parent and what is expected of them.

No matter what you and your former spouse think of each other, your children have the right to know and have a relationship with both of you. You cannot control or change each other, or monitor your children's relationships with each other. All you can do is to be the best influence you can be for them. Let your children have their own experiences of the other parent, which will not be the same as your experience. You might explain to the children: "Dad [or Mom] and I are two different people. We see things differently. When you are with me, this is what I expect of you. When you are with your dad [or mom], his [or her] rules will probably be different." This teaches children to respect individual differences.

It cannot be left up to one parent to decide whether the other is worthy of seeing the children. Both parents have the right to see them. If one parent is uncooperative, it may become necessary for the parent being denied access to obtain legal assistance: the counsel of an attorney, a legal clinic, or a law school (where free legal advice is frequently available). When a parent and child are not allowed time together, it is the child who is most hurt.

A parent says a child is too young to go

When a parent refuses visitation rights outside of his or her presence because the child is an infant or very young, I encourage that parent to talk about her (or his) apprehensions and feelings with the other parent. I wish to stress that both parents must cooperate so *their* child will not end up deprived of one parent. It is essential for parents to develop a parenting plan that allows the estranged parent to gradually reenter the child's life and to become an involved parent without traumatizing the child. If one parent is not familiar with caring for the child, I urge the primary caregiver to prepare an information sheet that includes schedules and instructions for the child's care.

Since many parents feel uncomfortable and tense about visiting their child in the other parent's home, parents must explore mutually acceptable alternatives; for example, until the child becomes comfortable with the estranged parent, they can meet in a neutral place with a neutral third person whom the child knows. Contact usually begins with frequent, short visits and progresses to longer periods until full access between parent and child has been established. Younger children need more frequent contact. A gradual reentry plan for them usually begins with a visit for several hours, several times a week, in a neutral setting (such as a park), with a familiar third person present, for several weeks. Then they meet for an entire day once a week, or semiweekly, for several weeks. Next they visit for one day and one night overnight for several weeks. When the child and parent are comfortable together, they share complete weekends, and may continue to increase the length of their contact.

Letting go for the first time is the hardest, but you and your child will get used to it. You may even come to enjoy the time off. It is wonderful being a parent but it is also a big responsibility. Sharing this responsibility with your child's other parent benefits both you and your child. The longer you wait to establish this, the harder it will be for your child.

Financial Issues

Financial issues are put before children's needs

It is not unusual for divorcing parents to become suspicious, anxious, and even panicky about the many financial issues that are raised during a divorce. The stresses can become overwhelming.

To parents who refuse or are hesitant to work out a parenting plan before the financial issues are settled, I must stress the importance of putting the children first. I strongly urge them to separate issues regarding their children from the financial ones, even though I realize that financial issues are very important.

Although parents are, understandably, very concerned about their future financial security and how they will survive, they should be *at least as* concerned about their children's emotional security. The financial settlement might take a long time, but it will get settled eventually. In the meantime, and at all times, children need some relief. They are not property; they don't come with the house. At the very least I urge parents to consider working out a temporary agreement that affords the family some structure and guidelines to follow through this difficult period.

One option for parents who cannot agree on financial issues is divorce mediation, during which time each parent can make a proposal for consideration. In the event that no agreement is reached through mediation, parents can each hire an attorney to handle the financial settlement. With their attorneys' help, parents may be able to reach a stipulated settlement between themselves. As a last resort, a judge can decide. No matter which way it goes, once the legal system is involved, neither parent is apt to feel that the financial settlement is fair.

Sometimes it can take years for financial issues to be settled. Regardless, *it is essential that parents cooperate regarding their children.* Children deserve and need a livable situation; they cannot be put on hold until the details of a financial settlement are decided.

A parent does not pay child support

When parents separate and divorce, less money is usually available since two separate households must be established. This puts a heavy financial burden on both parents.

One father of a three-year-old sadly described his situation. "I'm not working now and I can't pay child support, so my ex-wife won't let me see my son. I haven't seen him for four months, and Christmas is coming soon. I miss him very much. Is there anything I can do?"

It is a parental obligation to support the children, and child-support payments should be made promptly and regularly—but a parent's visitations should not be withheld if child support is not paid. This only hurts the children, for they are likely to feel abandoned and unloved by their parent. While child support can be made up, this type of hurt can stay with them forever.

Sometimes parents can afford to pay child support but refuse to for various reasons. In such cases, the custodial parent can seek assistance from state or local county child-support enforcement agencies to get support payments. Since each state is different, it is best to check in the telephone directory for the nearest office. In some areas the County District Attorney handles child-support enforcement, while in others it is the County Revenue Office that provides this service.

These child-support enforcement agencies utilize various mechanisms for collecting delinquent child support payments. For example, if the delinquent parent has a professional license, a commercial driver's license, or a business license with the Franchise Tax Board, it can be suspended until all delinquent child support payments have been paid; or if a parent is working, his or her weekly pay checks can be intercepted and payment made to the custodial parent.

Child-support enforcement agencies can also help with locating a delinquent parent, establishing paternity, and determining how much child support should be paid.

Child Safety Issues

A parent is concerned about the children's safety

Parents are sometimes worried about their children's safety in the hands of the other parent; they voice concerns such as: "The children are left unattended"; "They are not properly supervised"; "He [or she] doesn't use safety devices in the car while transporting the children." A parent may be concerned about the other parent's use of alcohol or illegal drugs. In such cases, I encourage parents to work together in providing a safe environment and adequate supervision for the children. Parents often agree on including one or more clauses into their parenting agreement that restrains one or both of them from exposing the children to any of these dangers. I urge parents to keep these agreements for their children's sake and to build trust between them as parents.

When one parent says that the child is, was, or would be in danger of physical or sexual abuse or kidnapping, or that serious threats have been made against the child's or the parent's life, or there has been extremely bizarre behavior on the part of the other parent—serious allegations have been made. The concerned parent must do everything necessary to protect the children.

When parents are willing, a plan can be developed that includes some safeguards to protect the children, such as restraining orders against the use of alcohol or drugs in the children's presence, or against transporting the child without a car seat or seat belt, or against leaving the child unsupervised. Some parents agree to let the other parent visit, but only in their presence or in the presence of a neutral third party. When one parent expresses a great deal of concern, I suggest that he or she ask the court to appoint an investigator or a psychiatrist to evaluate all family members. I also urge parents to consider individual or family counseling.

One parent is concerned about a child's treatment by the other parent

It is not uncommon for divorcing parents to be concerned about the way a child is being treated by the other parent. For example, one parent told me that her twelve-year-old daughter came back after visiting her father and complained that her father called her stupid, and stated that she didn't want to see him anymore. I explained to this mother that parents differ widely in the way they handle their children; some are very strict, others highly permissive. Although I am strongly against calling children names, I cautioned my client about the harm in talking to her daughter against the other parent or in pointing out the other parent's faults. This could aggravate the problem and harm the child in the end.

When a child is upset and complains about how he or she has been treated by the other parent, I suggest that the child be encouraged to talk to the other parent directly. I tell the concerned parent that it is best not to interfere in their relationship and to let them work it out between themselves. That way, the other parent is less likely to blame the former spouse for the problem, and will have to deal with the child directly.

If your child is complaining to you about the other parent, it is possible that this same child is complaining about you to *that* parent. Some children manipulate both parents in this way, telling each what they think that parent wants to hear. This usually happens when parents are not cooperating with each other. Children are less likely to try this form of manipulation if parents work together.

A parent takes a child away

Child snatching is a serious federal offense. Some unfortunate children have lived nightmarish lives, snatched back and forth by their parents, sometimes not seeing one of their parents for many years. Once kidnapped children are located, they are usually taken from the parent who snatched them and awarded to the other parent. The parent who took them is usually allowed only monitored visitation rights.

If a parent is feeling desperate and talking of resorting to kidnapping, I plead on behalf of the children that he or she seeks both legal and therapeutic counseling.

Psychological Issues

A parent has difficulty accepting the divorce

A parent who does not want a divorce is often in great pain. He or she may try to pressure the other parent for reconciliation, and if that fails, may threaten to take the children away, not support the children, or become physically abusive to the other parent.

My suggestion to the parent who is against the divorce is that he or she refrain from pressuring the other parent to reconcile. This only puts the other parent on the defensive and interferes with the new relationship that must develop. I also suggest that threats of *all* kinds be avoided.

When one parent truly wants a divorce, there is nothing the other can do except learn from his or her own mistakes in the marriage and cooperate in raising the children. It can be helpful if each parent accepts some responsibility for causing the divorce. This enables each to become a stronger person, instead of feeling like a powerless victim.

If a parent is too upset to work together regarding the children, professional counseling is in order. It can help that parent sort things out and put the situation into perspective. As painful as this time is, I encourage parents to use this crisis as a turning point for growth in self-awareness, self-respect, and self-control.

A child has difficulty accepting the divorce

It is not unusual for children to be upset by a divorce. Most children want their parents to love each other and to stay together. Children go through various stages of mourning after a divorce, much as adults do.

One way to help children accept the divorce is by letting them express their feelings. Let them know that although their parents will not be living together anymore, the children will be loved and taken care of by both parents. Children should be given permission by both of their parents to love both parents and all the people in their life who are good to them, including grandparents, stepparents, relatives, and friends on both sides of the family.

Children can be given simple explanations or reasons for the divorce without blame being placed on anyone, such as, "Daddy and I have problems and we cannot work them out," or "Mommy and I aren't happy together." Children do not have to hear all the details—and in many cases, they shouldn't. The main thing that children want and need to hear is that they will still be loved and cared for.

If a child is having extreme difficulty—exhibiting symptoms such as problems eating or sleeping, acting out, withdrawal, depression, self-destructive or suicidal tendencies, or alcohol or drug abuse—I strongly urge parents to seek professional psychological help for them as soon as possible.

One parent feels manipulated by the other

After separation and divorce, some parents are very sensitive about being manipulated by the other parent, especially if this was an issue for them during the marriage.

One mother explained her feelings to me this way: During their twelve-year marriage, she thought of her husband as dreadful, only interested in his career. Since the separation, she felt he was trying to manipulate her through the children. He was seeing the children two evenings a week for dinner and three weekends a month. If the children had an activity during his time with them, he was willing to change his visits providing the mother make up the lost visiting time to him out of her own time. If the children were sick and missed their time with him, he expected the mother to make it up at another time. She resented his expectations very much. "I want to be able to plan things too," she lamented.

I explained to her that it is important for parents to be flexible and willing to make occasional changes to accommodate the children so they can continue their activities. Juggling schedules can be frustrating even when parents live together, and it becomes more complicated after separation. Parents can get extremely protective of their time with the children because they are frightened of losing them and of being dominated or manipulated by the other parent. As difficult as this situation may seem at times, I told her, it would be far worse for the children if their father did not want to see them at all.

Even if a parent does not want to make changes to accommodate the other parent, I try to make it understood that some flexibility is important, especially for special occasions or unusual circumstances; otherwise, the children are the losers. Whenever possible, a parent should avoid making plans for the children on the other parent's time. Getting even with the other parent for what happened during the marriage by being rigid about schedules will end up hurting the children most of all. On the other hand, a parent does not have to allow herself or himself to become a martyr or to be constantly inconvenienced by the other parent.

Lifestyle Issues

Parents live far apart

When parents live far apart, I emphasize the importance of developing a parenting plan that affords the children as much time as possible with each parent. When children are of school age, I usually suggest a plan in which the children live during the school year with one parent, and live with the other during most of summer, winter, and spring vacations. Occasionally a parent will ask for six months each year with the children. This schedule, however, often disrupts the children's education and makes it more difficult for them to adjust.

I encourage parents to explore ways for the children to spend most of the winter and spring vacations with the parent who does not have physical custody during the school year. For example, a schedule could allow children to spend alternate Christmases and Easters with the parent who does not have physical custody. That parent would get the children for the entire winter vacation and the entire spring vacation on alternate years. During in-between years, the children would be with that parent from the day after Christmas until the day before school commences and for one week during the spring vacation—excluding the weekend of Easter—from Friday to the following Friday.

When a parent happens to be visiting the area where the children are living, additional arrangements for contact with the children should be made. I also encourage regular weekly telephone contact as a way of maintaining communication between visits.

At some point, the children may want to reverse this basic schedule and live during the school year for one or several years with the other parent. It is natural for them to want this, and neither parent should see their desire for change as a tragedy. It should come from the children's own desire and not because they have been pressured by one of the parents, which could create tremendous pressure for them. If your children ever desire to reverse or otherwise alter the schedule, it would be beneficial for both of you to discuss this, and if the change is agreed upon, to give the children your permission to leave. They then won't feel like traitors to the parent they are leaving behind.

A parent is remarrying or lives with a significant other

It can be extremely upsetting for some divorcing or divorced parents when the other parent remarries or is living with another man or woman. One distraught mother explained her feelings this way: "My husband left us for another woman. Now he wants to see my son, and he wants Robert to attend his wedding. I refuse to let Robert go there as long as his father is living with that woman, and Robert doesn't want to go to the wedding because he knows how much I've been hurt."

Even though a parent may feel very upset about her or his ex-spouse's new relationships, the child still has the right to spend time with the other parent and to participate in his or her life. It is unwise to saddle a child with having to protect a "wounded" parent. Instead, children should be encouraged *not* to take sides.

Some parents want to limit or restrict their children's contact with the other parent because that parent is living with a significant other. No matter how you feel personally about people living together, each person must make this decision for her- or himself. When a parent is concerned about this issue, I offer reassurance by verifying that the children have their own beds, sleep separately from their parents, and are not exposed to adult sexual activity.

A parent is homosexual

After a divorce or separation in which one parent is homosexual, the heterosexual parent is sometimes concerned about the children spending time with the homosexual parent.

One mother told me that after five years of marriage, her husband revealed that he was gay. "He hid it from me entirely and I'm very angry that he deceived me, for I would not have had a child with him if I had known." After the separation, she was worried about her three-year-old son being around his father's gay friends. She was afraid he might be harmed or might become gay, too. Her husband promised he would be discreet, but she mistrusted him and wondered if she should prevent him from seeing their son.

My response to her, and to all parents in similar situations, is that a homosexual parent has rights to see his or her children; children need a relationship with *both* parents. Children do not "become gay" because a parent is gay. A heterosexual parent should not keep a child from a homosexual parent or try to control which friends that parent sees.

It is vital that both homosexual *and* heterosexual parents are discreet around children, and it is unlikely that any parent would allow his or her children to be molested. The less worry, attention, and energy around this issue, the less of an issue it will be for the children, and the less chance it will affect them negatively.

Parental Relationship Issues

One or both parents are angry and hostile toward the other

It takes time for painful feelings to heal, and in time most parents become more reasonable and predictable. In the meantime, I urge parents to keep as calm as possible around their children. Parents need to learn how to work together, for children *can* recover from a divorce when they are not being pulled back and forth or exposed to constant hostility between parents.

If parents are preoccupied with blaming each other, they are not learning from the past, and their chances of making a better life for themselves and their children are diminished. When there is much hostility between parents, or much bitterness on the part of one or both parents, I encourage them to seek individual or divorce counseling. In a counseling setting, it is possible for parents to discuss feelings and to begin to realize their mutual responsibility for the way their relationship turned out—a difficult but healing process.

Physical or verbal abuse between parents has been a problem

There are serious negative consequences to children of continual conflict between parents. Memories of watching negative parental interaction can remain with children for the rest of their lives. When physical or verbal abuse has been part of the parents' relationship, or when parents tend to inflame each other or fight in front of the children, it is essential to establish ground rules that minimize parental contact during the exchange of the children. I urge all parents to contain their anger and not to argue or fight in front of their children.

While they may not be physically hurt by the abusive parent, children do suffer abuse when they witness domestic violence. If your ex-spouse is abusive or threatens abuse, I suggest calling the Child Abuse Hotline in your area to find help and support for your child. This number can be obtained from Directory Assistance. The physical abuse of another person is a criminal offense, and it is prosecuted by the court. In domestic violence emergencies, dial 911 for the local police department. They can intervene in a situation and put you in touch with other resources.

Assistance for victims of domestic violence is sparse in many parts of the country. Some areas provide temporary shelter to house and protect women and children, and some organizations offer legal and emotional counseling. Through the civil courts, you can file a restraining order against a partner to prevent harassment and domestic violence.

California leads the nation in services to victims of domestic violence. In Los Angeles County, for example, if a person calls the police department to report domestic violence, a hearing officer is on duty at all times to assist the victim in obtaining an immediate restraining order. Hopefully, as our collective consciousness rises about the epidemic proportions of domestic violence, more states will provide these much needed services.

———

When a marriage come to an end, even the coolest-headed parents are faced with difficult problems to solve and tremendous challenges to overcome. They have themselves and their own lives to worry about, they have their children to raise, and they have a potentially sensitive relationship with the other parent to develop and maintain. As difficult as it may sometimes seem, I hope love and concern for the children will strengthen parents' resolve to cooperate with each other and be the best parents they can be.

10

Where to Find Help

On airplane flights, passengers are instructed in the emergency use of oxygen masks should extreme loss of pressure occur in the cabin. Parents traveling with children are told to place the mask on themselves first, then to assist children with their masks. The reason is obvious: if the parent were to lose consciousness, there would be no one to help the children.

The same concept could be applied to parents and children after separation and divorce. Parents need to take immediate steps to help themselves maintain balance and keep their sanity. If parents become unconscious of everything but their own pain, they lose the ability to consider their children's needs. Parents owe it to themselves and their children to get psychological help and/or legal advice, and to create a support network of some kind that will help them come to terms with the situation. They need to maintain their responsibility as parents.

In time, everyone can recover, heal, and even do very well after a divorce. The recovery process usually takes two or three years, and it may take longer. During this time, parents who have great difficulty coping need to seek help for themselves so that they can take proper care of their children.

The children may need help also. A few sessions with a counselor or therapist can make an amazing difference. The following true story (see *References,* 6) is an example of how quickly a child can respond to and benefit from counseling and mediation, even in extremely difficult cicumstances.

Halli was a bright, sensitive girl of almost eleven. Her parents and their attorneys were referred to me directly from the courtroom where the parents were litigating over custody and visitation issues.

They had separated when Halli was seven, and Halli's mother had remarried when Halli was eight.

During the first conference, Halli's mother, father, and stepfather, as well as the parents' attorneys, were present. After I briefly explained the mediation process, the attorneys waited outside while I talked to the parents, Martha and Hal. Martha began, "Halli refuses to see her father. I haven't told her not to go. I can't push her out the door." She stated that she was concerned for her child and had been taking Halli to a child psychologist for the past month. "Her psychologist feels she shouldn't be forced until she can work it out. I want her to see her father."

I asked Martha if Halli had given her any reason why she didn't wish to see her father. "She's mad at him for leaving us. Our lifestyle was to stay married and not to have extramarital sex. Halli is upset about Hal's constant changes in girlfriends. When they break up, Halli believes he is hurting them the way he hurt me." Martha believed Hal should wait until Halli had accepted the divorce and not force her to go with him. "I want them both to feel good about it," she said. She indicated her concern about the negative consequences of the divorce on her child, because Halli had seen and heard a lot of verbal and physical abuse between Hal and Martha.

Hal told me he loved Halli very much and wanted to share his life with her. "I can't work on my relationship with her if I don't have any contact. I don't want to wait a long time to see her. Martha doesn't encourage her to see me. Separateness doesn't lead to resolving this situation. And I don't have a flow of women. I lived first with one woman and now with another woman, whom I plan to marry—only two different women." Hal added with great feeling, "I want to see my daughter on a regular basis. If I get to spend time with her, I am confident we will work it out. If I don't get to see her regularly, I believe a change of custody is necessary now, otherwise this will keep happening. I'll give Martha the same visitation rights she would give me."

I talked to them about their mutual responsibility for the problem, about the importance of them cooperating to correct the situation for Halli's sake, and about the negative consequences for children when a serious rift develops between a parent and child. I suggested that Halli be included in the mediation process, and presented the possibility of Hal's participating in a few counseling sessions with Halli and her psychologist. Hal was against participating in counseling, as the psychologist had recommended that Halli not be forced to see her father, but both parents agreed to return with Halli the following week.

On the day of their appointment, I explained the purpose of the meeting to Halli, then asked her parents to wait outside. Most children sit quietly and wait for my first question, but Halli immediately began airing her resentments about her father. "He goes from lady to lady even when he was married to my mother." I asked her how she knew this, and she said her mother had told her so. Halli continued, "If I start with that I will have a terrible life. This lady will be left like a dead rose." Halli's eyes filled with tears as she told me that her father had punched her mother in the stomach when she was in her mother's womb. Again, she said her mother had told her this.

"When I was five years old, my father punished me by putting me to bed because he wanted me to clean my room. He never did love me. He lied on the court papers." I asked Halli how she knew this, and she told me that she and her mother had read them and that her father had contradicted himself.

Halli said she never believed her father loved her. "When he left I thought he would come back, but he didn't. If he had really loved me, he wouldn't have left me." She added, "It's a lie that my mother's trying to put words in my mouth."

I asked Halli what made her decide not to see her father. "We went away for the weekend to a hotel, and my father had sex with that lady. I know because I came into the room and she had her bikini top unfastened. After that I didn't want to see him anymore. I think he's trying to threaten my mother by taking her to court. He doesn't want to see me. He has no love. He thinks sex is love. He never took care of me when I was a baby. Do you get the point?"

I asked Halli what the worst thing was that her father had done to her. "He left me. It's in my heart and in my mother's and it never comes out until we talk to someone." I asked Halli where she felt the hurt in her body, and she replied, "It makes me want to cry. It feels like, you know, when you're cold." She shivered. "Like that." Halli continued, "Every day he'd beat my mother up. I would see him punch her."

I asked Halli if she would give me permission to share what we talked about with her father, and Halli replied, "Good. I want to see how he will react to the lies he's telling and to what I say, and what he's going to do when his girlfriend is in here." She added, "I don't want to see my father's face. I didn't look at him in the waiting room. I want him to know what it's like to be hurt. He has never been hurt. He left my mother and left another woman like a dead rose. He'll leave this lady too." I asked Halli if she thought she could ever forgive her father, and she replied, "I can never forgive him for the way he hurt my heart."

When I asked Halli if she had told her father about how she felt, she replied, "I've never told my father all these things."

Instead of bringing both parents and Mike, Halli's stepfather, and Kay, Hal's friend, in at this point, which I would normally have done, I brought in only Hal so that Halli and her father could have a chance to be together alone. I also thought it would be easier for Hal to accept Halli's feelings if Martha were not present. I explained this to Martha, and she accepted my decision.

When Hal came into the room, Halli went to the far end of the room, turning her back on him. I told Hal that I would be summarizing Halli's feelings and that it might be difficult for him to hear what Halli had to say. I explained that feelings don't have a right or wrong, they are just the way they are, and that sometimes when feelings are expressed they come loose. They can then change and a closer relationship can develop. I summarized what Halli and I had talked about. When I finished, Hal told Halli how amazed and sad he was to hear how much hurt he had caused her.

Halli waited outside while I discussed the situation with the adults. Again, I strongly suggested that Hal take part in at least one session with Halli's psychologist. He reluctantly agreed to give it a try and to postpone further visitation until after his meeting with the psychologist. All present agreed to return in one month to evaluate what progress had been made.

One month later, Halli walked into my office, smiling. "Things are working out," she announced. "I'm seeing my father again. I might forgive him. After we talked about it, he knows what I want and I know what he wants."

I asked Halli, "What do you want?"

"When I'm with him, I don't want him to sleep with any ladies. I want them to have separate beds."

"What does your father want?"

Halli smiled. "He wants to see me. He wants a better relationship with me. He wants me to forgive him. He found out he hurt me more than he thought he did. He apologized, and I forgave him."

Again Halli gave permission for me to share what we talked about with her parents. Martha told me that a big change had taken place in Halli. "She is so happy now."

Hal announced to everyone that he was planning to get married that summer, and that he wanted Halli to attend his wedding. Halli smiled approvingly. I asked Halli jokingly, "*Then* will it be all right for your father to sleep with Kay?" Without hesitation, Halli smiled and answered, "Yes!"

Children are extremely resilient. They can heal rather quickly once the pressure is eased or their situation changes for the better. Usually, a resolution between their parents that brings an end to hostilities and some constructive cooperation will restore a kernel of security in children's lives.

Adults need a wider and more complex support network. Family and friends can help, but sometimes a person is too isolated, or the problem lies so deep that the trained care of a professional is best. At such times divorcing adults owe it to themselves—and their children—to seek out and use the resources in their community.

On the following pages are listed various kinds of services available to separated, divorcing, or divorced parents. These include psychological services, emergency services, legal services, parent support groups, conciliation courts, and family court mediation services, and conflict resolution and mediation associations and agencies. On pages 199–203 are listed books that parents might find helpful.

Emergency Services for Families

Immediate help for serious problems such as spouse battering, child abuse, child molestation, and rape can be found through

- local police departments

- battered women's shelters

- child protective services

Help for serious psychological disturbances can be obtained through county mental-health agencies.

For problems with addictions, self-help groups such as Alcoholics Anonymous, Narcotics Anonymous, and Gamblers Anonymous are available in many communities for treating specific problems and are listed in the yellow pages under "Service Organizations."

For hotlines and specialized social services, call directory information or look under "Social Service Organizations" in the yellow pages.

In addition to these resources, many clergy are trained in pastoral counseling and can provide counseling themselves or give referrals for help elsewhere.

Psychological Services

The following professional associations can provide information regarding trained marriage, family, and child counselors; social workers; and psychologists and psychiatrists in your area.

American Association of Marriage and Family Therapy
1100 17th Street NW
Washington DC 20036   (202) 452-0109

American Psychiatric Association
1400 K Street NW
Washington DC 20005   (202) 682-6000

American Psychological Association
750 First Street NE
Washington DC 20005 (202) 336-5500

National Association of Social Workers, Inc.
545 Eighth Avenue
New York NY 10018 (212) 947-5000

Legal Services

Referrals for legal advice can be obtained from local county bar associations, through the yellow pages listed under "Divorce" and through the American Bar Association:

American Bar Association
750 North Lake Shore Drive
Chicago IL 60611 (312) 988-5000

I suggest that parents ask for a referral to a *family law* attorney. Parents are wise to shop around until they find an attorney whose goal is to help parents settle their differences rather than to litigate, especially when litigation is not in the children's and parents' best interests. Many fine and ethical attorneys realize that family law is not like criminal, corporate, or other law. When the divorce is over, the litigants (parents) have to work together regarding their children. It is therefore important that attorneys try to deescalate the conflict whenever possible and to help parents settle their differences.

Parent Support Groups

Joint Custody Association
10606 Wilkins Avenue
Los Angeles CA 90024 (310) 475-5352

National Council for Children's Rights
220 I Street NE
Washington DC 20002 (202) 547-6227

Parents Without Partners International Office
401 N. Michigan Avenue
Chicago IL 60611   (312) 644-6610

Conciliation Courts and Family Court Mediation Services

To find the current status of conciliation courts in your area, inquire at your local courthouse, or contact the Association of Family and Conciliation Courts:

Association of Family and Conciliation Courts
329 West Wilson
Madison WI 53703   (608) 251-4001

Conflict-Resolution and Mediation Associations and Agencies

American Arbitration Association
140 West 51st Street
New York NY 10020   (212) 484-4000

American Bar Association
Special Committee on Alternative Means of Dispute Resolution
1800 M Street NW
Washington DC 20036   (202) 331-2200

Association of Family and Conciliation Courts
329 West Wilson
Madison WI 53703   (608) 251-4001

National Council for Children's Rights
220 I Street NE
Washington DC 20002   (202) 547-6227

11

How to Help Your Child Through Your Divorce: A Summary

At a time when divorcing parents are faced with no limit of problems, there are also the children to be cared for. Children are by nature needy, dependent, and vulnerable, and they are all the more so following separation and divorce. Major problems can be averted and children can heal from the divorce if their needs are met.

Children Need Both Parents

If children are to have a good outcome and succeed after divorce, they cannot be put on hold while parents rebuild their lives. They need a nurturing relationship with both parents in the meantime.

Even if a child has a close and loving relationship with one parent, if the child doesn't also experience a satisfying relationship with the other parent, the child's self-esteem will suffer. Children must have the right to have and to build a relationship with both parents, and have significant time with both.

Children can recover from and do well after a divorce *if* their parents work together to help them. Even if parents don't like each other, they can learn to work together for the good of the child. They are no longer *marriage partners*, but they are still *parent partners*.

Children tend to do best after separation and divorce when both parents are involved in their lives. Children who do worst are those exposed to continual parental conflict and those who lose a parent as a result of the divorce. Even sporadic visits are better for a child than no visits.

Children Need a Healthy Environment

To thrive after a divorce, children need a supportive and caring environment. They need reassurance that they will continue to be cared for, no matter what happens. And they must get that care— from kind and loving people.

Children need to be protected from parental conflict, arguments, and violence. They need protection from physical, emotional, and sexual abuse. They also need protection from the pressure of having to choose where they want to live.

To develop trust and self-confidence, children need reasonable limits set for their behavior, and sufficient warning before disciplinary action is taken. And they need an environment that allows them freedom to express their concerns and feelings, even negative ones.

Outside Help Is Available

If you and your ex-spouse find you just can't work things out between you, help is available. In divorce mediation, a neutral third party—a mediator—will help you discuss issues regarding the children and explore ways of resolving your differences. Through mediation, many parents are able to reach an agreement and avoid a costly court battle. Court litigation over the child-custody issues should be a last resort, because it often leads to more dissatisfaction and hostility between parents, and usually results in more problems for the children.

There are some warning signs of a child in trouble: anxiety, depression, bedwetting, eating or sleeping disorders, school problems, overaggressive behavior, alcohol or drug abuse, and other unusual, persistent symptoms. If you notice any of these in your child, seek help before the child sustains lasting psychological damage.

Guidelines for Creating a Healthy Environment

You can create a safer, more secure, and more harmonious environment for your children by following these guidelines:

- Refrain from saying anything derogatory about the other parent in front of the children.

- Refrain from bringing up past grievances about the other parent to the children.

- Refrain from discussing financial and legal issues and disputes with the children.

- Refrain from saying anything that might discourage the children from spending time with the other parent, and from pressuring them to take sides against the other parent.

- Be willing to share the children with the other parent, and work out a parenting plan as soon as possible after the separation.

- Be willing to cooperate and communicate with the other parent regarding the children.

- Encourage the children to have a close relationship with parents, stepparents, and grandparents.

Characteristics of a Healthy Restructured Family

After divorce, the restructured family can be whole and healthy. The characteristics of a healthy restructured family can serve as a guide and model for you to strive for.

In a healthy restructured family, there is a willingness of the parents to set the past aside and focus on the children's needs. This is accompanied by an ability and willingness to communicate regarding the children, and a willingness to share time and responsibility for raising them.

Parents of a healthy restructured family respect the other parent's privacy and promote the other parent's relationship with the children. They are also willing to cooperate in crisis situations and to seek outside help when it is needed.

———

It's not too late to change your behavior and your attitude to help your child. Children are resilient and can heal quickly once their situation improves. I wish you and yours a complete healing and a bright future.

Suggested Reading List

Books About Children of Divorce

The Day the Loving Stopped. Julie List. New York: Fawcett, 1986.
   List kept this journal as a child, when her parents divorced. It is a devastating account of the typical divorce and its effect on children.

Helping Your Children Cope with Divorce. Edward Teyber. Lexington MA: Heath, 1994.

Helping Your Child Through Your Divorce. Florence Bienenfeld. Alameda: Hunter House, 1994.
   This book offers parents practical guidelines for easing the pain and developing a positive outcome for children after divorce. It contains a wealth of information on mediation, parenting plans, and joint-custody, and includes case studies and children's drawings about divorce.

Parents' Book About Divorce. Richard A. Gardner. Cresskill NJ: Creative Therapeutics, 1991.
   In this book, a psychiatrist gives realistic guidance for parents who are having troubles with their children because of divorce. Dr. Gardner offers a positive approach and a comprehensive treatment of complex issues.

Second Chances: Men, Women and Children a Decade After Divorce. Judith S. Wallerstein and Sandra Blakeslee. New York: Ticknor and Fields, 1990.
   Researchers reinterviewed all members of 60 families ten years after divorce, and this book is an account of the findings.

Surviving the Breakup. Judith S. Wallerstein and Joan Berlin Kelly. New York: Basic Books, 1990.
> This book has valuable information on the impact of divorce on children and on what factors affect children's ability to cope.

Your Child's Self-Esteem. Dorothy C. Briggs. New York: Doubleday, 1975.
> This book is not about divorce per se, but the insights into child behavior and development will help parents deal with their children in difficult times.

Books for Children of Divorce

The Boys' and Girls' Book About Divorce. Richard A. Gardner. New York: Bantam, 1971.
> Directed to children age 8 and older, this book attempts to help them understand and cope with the experience of divorce.

The Boys' and Girls' Book About One-Parent Families. Richard A. Gardner. Cresskill NJ: Creative Therapeutics, 1983.

The Boys and Girls Book About Stepfamilies. Richard A. Gardner. Cresskill NJ: Creative Therapeutics, 1985.
> This book is written on a sixth-grade level.

Dinosaurs' Divorce: A Guide for Changing Families. Laurence K. Brown and Marc T. Brown. New York: Little Brown, 1988.

The Divorce Workbook: A Guide for Kids and Families. Sally B. Ives. Burlington VT: Waterfront Books, 1985.
> This is a useful therapeutic tool to help children communicate their feelings.

How to Get It Together When Your Parents Are Coming Apart. Arlene Kramer Richards and Irene Willis. Summit NJ: Willard Press, 1986.
> This book aims at helping teenagers deal with their parents' divorce.

It's Not the End of the World. Judy Blume. New York: Bradbury Press, 1982.

> This book, for children ages 10 to 14, tells the story of a girl who schemes to get her divorced parents back together.

Mom and Dad Don't Live Together Anymore. Kathy Stinson. Buffalo NY: Firefly Books, 1984.

My Mom and Dad Are Getting a Divorce. Florence Bienenfeld. St. Paul MN: EMC Corporation, 1984. (Available only from EMC, 300 York Avenue, St. Paul MN 55101, for $6.20 including postage.)

> This colorfully illustrated book is written for children from 4 to 12. It helps children express feelings and helps parents deal with those feelings. Endorsed by the Association of Family Conciliation Courts.

One More Time. Louis Baum. New York: William Morrow and Co., 1992.

Talking About Divorce and Separation: A Dialogue Between Parent and Child. Earl A. Grollman. New York: Beacon Press, 1975.

> This book helps young children and their parents discuss the experience and feelings that accompany divorce.

Two Homes to Live In: A Child's Eye View of Divorce, Barbara Shooks-Hazen. New York: Human Science Press, 1983.

What Kind of Family Is This? A Book About Stepfamilies. Chicago: Children's Press, 1985.

Books Regarding Shared Custody

Joint-Custody Handbook. Miriam G. Cohen. Philadelphia: Running Press, 1991.

> A series of reports from the trenches by parents who opted for joint-custody arrangements in the 1970s.

Joint-Custody and Shared Parenting. edited by Jay Folberg. New York: Gilford Press, 1991.

> A compilation of writings on the legal, social, and practical aspects of joint-custody, including a survey of custody across the U.S., with particular emphasis on joint-custody and co-parenting.

Mom's House, Dad's House: Making Shared Custody Work. Isolina Ricci. New York: Macmillan, 1982.

> This sensitively written book articulates practical and systematic guidelines for parents who are contemplating divorce, are involved in divorce litigation, or are already divorced. Persuasive arguments support the pioneering idea that divorced parents can cooperate and build two homes for their children, even when they are not on friendly terms.

Books for Divorced Fathers

101 Ways to Be a Long-Distance Super Dad. George Newman. San Jose CA: R & E Publishers, 1981.

Books on Stepparenting

Stepfamilies: Myths and Realities. Emily Visher and John Visher. New York: Carol Publishing Group, 1980.

The Stepfamily: Living, Loving and Learning. Elizabeth A. Einstein. E. Einstein, 1994.

Books On Divorce and Personal Growth

Crazy Time: Surviving Divorce. Abigail Trafford. New York: Bantam, 1984.

Creative Divorce, Mel Krantzer. New York: NAL Dutton, 1975.

Growing Through Divorce. Jim Smoke. Eugene OR: Bantam, 1986.

How to Survive the Loss of a Love. Melba Colgrove, Harold Bloomfield, Peter McWilliams, et al. Los Angeles: Prelude Press, 1993.
Written by a psychologist, psychiatrist and a poet, this book offers first aid for those suffering from emotional hurt.

Turning Points: How People Change Through Crisis and Commitment, Ellen Goodman. New York: Fawcett, 1982.

References

1. *Marriage and Divorce Today Newsletter,* report of a presentation made by Deborah Ann Leupnitz, Ph.D., to the Sixty-second Annual Meeting of the Orthopsychiatric Association, New York City, May 6, 1985.

2. Federick W. Ilfeld, Jr., M.D., Holly Zingale Ilfeld, M.A., and John R. Alexander, J.D., "Does Joint Custody Work? A First Look at Outcome Data of Relitigation," *American Journal of Psychiatry,* January 1982.

3. Isolina Ricci, Statewide Coordinator, Family Court Services, Judicial Council of California named the combining of both functions "Confluent-Mediation." Lecture: Association of Family Conciliation Courts Winter Conference, Ft. Lauderdale FL, December 4, 1981.

4. J. Bowlby, "Grief and Mourning in Infancy and Early Childhood." *Psycho-Analytic Study of the Child,* 1960, 15:6052.

5. Judith Wallerstein, Ph.D. Paper presented at the Third Annual Family Law Colloquium, Los Angeles, CA, November 1979.

6. Persia Woolley. *The Custody Handbook.* New York: Summit Books, 1979, 213.

7. Florence Bienenfeld, "How Child Custody Mediation Can Help Children," in *Family Therapy News,* July/August 1983.

Index

Hunter House
GROWTH AND RECOVERY WORKBOOKS FOR CHILDREN

These workbooks give children a safe place to explore and work through traumas and hurts. Each has 32 pages of exercises that are balanced between writing and drawing and are keyed to the phases and goals of therapy.

I AM A SURVIVOR is for children who have survived a natural disaster such as a flood, tornado, hurricane, fire, or earthquake (ages 9–12). **I SAW IT HAPPEN** is for children who have witnessed a traumatic event such as a car accident, a shooting at a school, or other violence (ages 9–12). **NO MORE HURT** is a therapy workbook that provides children who have been physically or sexually abused a safe place to explore their feelings (ages 9–12). **LIVING WITH MY FAMILY** helps children traumatized by domestic violence and family fights identify and express their fears (ages 9–12). **SOMEONE I LOVE DIED** is for children who have lost a loved one and are dealing with grief (ages 9–12). **A SEPARATION IN MY FAMILY** is for children whose parents are separating or have already separated or divorced (ages 9–12). **DRINKING AND DRUGS IN MY FAMILY** is for children with family members who engage in regular alcohol and substance abuse (ages 9–12).

MY OWN THOUGHTS AND FEELINGS FOR YOUNG GIRLS is for problems of depression, low self-esteem, family conflict, maladjustment, and nonspecific dysfunction in young girls (ages 6–10). **MY OWN THOUGHTS AND FEELINGS FOR YOUNG BOYS** is for problems of depression, low self-esteem, family conflict, maladjustment, and nonspecific dysfunction in young boys (ages 6–10). **MY OWN THOUGHTS AND FEELINGS ON STOPPING THE HURT** is for young children who may have suffered physical or emotional abuse (ages 6–10).

Each workbook comes with a Therapist's Guide: a removable four-page overview of the content and focus of the workbook, with page-by-page thumbnail explanations of each activity and helpful references to *Trauma in the Lives of Children* for more detailed information on each area (see book description on following page). Each workbook is also available as a Practitioner Pack. Packs include a workbook, guide, the entire text on double-sided cards, and a site license to make multiple copies.

A selection of Behavioral Science Book Service

Workbooks $9.95 each ... Practitioner Packs $17.95 each
Workbook Library (one of each title—10 total) $75.00
10-Pack (10 copies of a single title) $70.00

Prices subject to change

Printed in the USA
CPSIA information can be obtained
at www.ICGtesting.com
JSHW082202140824
68134JS00014B/389

9 780897 931687